THE MYSTERIOUS TIMES

STRANGE STORIES OF 30 REAL-LIFE MYSTERIES

MELISSA HECKSCHER AND THE STAFF OF *THE MYSTERIOUS TIMES*

THE MYSTERIOUS TIMES

ESTABLISHED 1872

Published by Tangerine Press,
an imprint of Scholastic Inc
557 Broadway
New York, NY 10012

10 9 8 7 6 5 4 3 2 1

ISBN 0-439-67652-5

Printed and bound in China

INTRODUCTION

EVERYBODY LOVES A GOOD MYSTERY

Have you ever seen a ghost? Have you ever heard the phone ring, guessed who was calling, and been right? Have you ever looked up into the sky and wondered: Is there anyone out there?

WE HAVE.

Do you ever suspect that there are lost cities buried deep underwater, black holes swirling in outer space, or giant creatures lurking undiscovered in our planet's lakes and oceans?

WE DO.

Did you know that a dapper, polite thief once jumped out of a plane with a bag full of stolen cash, or that a 16-year-old boy convinced the world he was an airline pilot?

WE'LL TELL YOU ABOUT IT.

The reporters, editors, and photojournalists at *The Mysterious Times* have been covering strange, sometimes unbelievable, events for more than 100 years.

We were there when a ship called the *Mary Celeste* was found sailing the ocean without a crew. We were there when the people of Roswell, New Mexico, claimed a spaceship landed in their backyard. And we were there when residents of the Scottish town of Loch Ness spotted a creature that looked like a massive serpent swimming in their lake.

Were the reports true? Did these bizarre things actually happen? Nobody knows for sure.

This book presents 30 of history's most notorious mysteries. It includes stories of still unsolved crimes, unusual animals, unidentified flying objects, seemingly magical events, and other unexplained happenings.

Our staff has attempted to provide all the facts to help you make sense of the stories. We've polled our readers, conducted interviews, and provided background information to offer you all the angles.

You may be a believer; then again, you may be a skeptic. Read on and decide for yourself. Just remember: There are some questions that simply can't be answered. Of course, without those questions, there would be no mysteries. And doesn't everyone love a good mystery?

WE DO.

PHOTO CREDITS

Front Cover: Center: Photograph of Stonehenge courtesy of Library of Congress, Prints and Photographs Division. Clockwise from upper left: Photograph of Harry Houdini courtesy of Library of Congress, Prints and Photographs Division. Photograph of Amelia Earhart courtesy of Library of Congress, Prints and Photographs Division. Photograph of Great Pyramids courtesy of National Archives. Illustration of mummy courtesy of Library of Congress, Prints and Photographs Division. Photograph of black hole courtesy of NASA/Chandra X-ray Observatory. Back Cover: Center: Illustration of alien as described by a UFO abductee courtesy of Phenomena Archives. Clockwise from upper left: Photograph of crop circle in a canola field, West Kennet, Wiltshire, England, courtesy of International Fortean Organization. Photograph of King Tutankhamun's golden casket courtesy of Library of Congress, Prints and Photographs Division. Photograph of the rover *Opportunity* courtesy of NASA/JPL/Malin Space Science Systems. Photograph of Harry Houdini and elephant Jenny courtesy of Library of Congress, Prints and Photographs Division. Page 5: Portrait of Captain Briggs and illustration of *Mary Celeste* courtesy of Peabody Essex Museum. Photograph of Brooklyn Bridge courtesy of Library of Congress, Prints and Photographs Division. Page 7: Photograph of Ignatius Donnelly by F. Gutekunst, courtesy of Minnesota Historical Society. Portrait of Plato and plan for Statue of Liberty courtesy of Library of Congress, Prints and Photographs Division. Page 8: Photograph of Atlantis: The Antediluvian World and map of Empire of Atlantis courtesy of Library of Congress, Prints and Photographs Division. Pages 9 and 10: Photographs of the Winchester House courtesy of Library of Congress, Prints and Photographs Division. Photograph of Albert Einstein courtesy of National Archives. Pages 11 and 12: Photograph of Butch Cassidy and Wild Bunch, Denver Public Library, Western History Collection. Illustration of Union Pacific Railroad courtesy of Library of Congress, Prints and Photographs Division. Page 13: Portrait of Charles Hoy Fort courtesy of International Fortean Organization (INFO). Illustration of alien courtesy of Phenomena Archives. Illustration of automobile courtesy of Library of Congress, Prints and Photographs Division. Page 14: Photograph of light on hill/early UFO sighting courtesy of International Fortean Organization (INFO). Photograph of a huge sturgeon courtesy of INFO Journal #54. Pages 15 and 16: Photographs and poster of Harry Houdini courtesy of Library of Congress, Prints and Photographs Division. Illustrations of "Mysterious Message Trick" courtesy of Nancy Leonard. Page 17: Photographs of Stonehenge and family listening to the radio courtesy of Library of Congress, Prints and Photographs Division. Page 18: Photographs of Stonehenge as is and reconstructed by S. Sutton courtesy of National Archives. "Rock's Route" map courtesy of Nancy Leonard. Pages 19 and 20: All photographs and illustrations courtesy of Library of Congress, Prints and Photographs Division. Page 21: Photographs of Khufu and Great Pyramids courtesy of National Archives. Page 22: Illustration of Hieroglyphs courtesy of Nancy Leonard. Painting of Pyramid of Kulkulcan at Chichen Itza courtesy of International Fortean Organization. Page 23: Photograph of Dr. J. B. Rhine and Dr. Louisa E. Rhine courtesy of *Washington Star*. Page 24: Illustrations of Zenar Cards courtesy of Nancy Leonard. Pages 25 to 26: All photographs courtesy of Library of Congress, Prints and Photographs Division. Page 27: Photograph of Loch Ness near Inverness, Scotland, courtesy of Library of Congress. Photograph of Loch Ness Monster by Robert Kenneth Wilson. Photograph of Bonnie and Clyde courtesy of Library of Congress, Prints and Photographs Division. Page 28: "Monster Word Search" and "Do You See Nessie?" games courtesy of Nancy Leonard. Pages 29 and 30: All photographs courtesy of Library of Congress, Prints and Photographs Division. Map of Amelia's final flight courtesy of Nancy Leonard. Pages 31 and 32: All illustrations courtesy of New York Public Library. Map courtesy of Library of Congress, Prints and Photographs Division. Page 33: Photograph of U.S. Navy fighter planes courtesy of US Navy/National Archives. Map of Bermuda Triangle courtesy of Nancy Leonard. Photograph of Slinky courtesy of Erika Rubel. Page 35: Photograph of Roswell Army Air Field both courtesy of Library of Congress, Prints and Photographs Division. Photograph of intelligence office with debris found near Roswell courtesy of Air Force Military Library. Photograph of Walker sign courtesy of National Archives. Page 36: Photograph illustrating "Is It a UFO?" courtesy of Library of Congress, Prints and Photographs Division. Pages 37 and 38: All photographs courtesy of Library of Congress, Prints and Photographs Division. Photograph of Mr. Potato Head courtesy of Dennis Martin. Pages 39 and 40: All photographs courtesy of National Archives. Photograph of Etch-A-Sketch courtesy of Erika Rubel. Page 41: All photographs courtesy of AP/Wideworld Photos. Page 42: All photographs courtesy of Library of Congress, Prints and Photographs Division. Page 43: Photograph of PanAmerican DC8 jet airliner courtesy of *Washington Star*. Photograph of Frank Abagnale courtesy of his office. Page 44: Photographs illustrating "How to Spot a Liar" courtesy of Lynne Yeamans. Page 45: Film still by Roger Patterson. Page 46: All photographs courtesy of AP/Wideworld Photos. "Whose Feet Are Those?" game courtesy of Nancy Leonard. Page 47: Illustration of the "Mothman" courtesy of Phyllis Benjamin. Photograph of bridge courtesy of WVDOT. Page 48: Photograph of Barn Owl courtesy of National Geographic. Pages 49 and 50: Photograph of search party and illustration of D. B. Cooper courtesy of Library of Congress, Prints and Photographs Division. Map of path of Flight 305 courtesy of Nancy Leonard. Illustration of Ping-Pong paddle courtesy of Raina Telgemeier. Pages 51 and 52: All photographs and illustrations courtesy of NOAA Photo Library/Department of Commerce. Pages 53 and 54: Photograph of barley formation and canola formation, Wiltshire, England, courtesy of International Fortean Organization. Page 55: Photograph of Isabella Stewart Gardner Museum courtesy of the Museum. *The Storm on the Sea of Galilee*, 1633 (oil on canvas) by Rembrandt Harmensz. van Rijn (1606-69), *The Concert*, c.1658-60 (oil on canvas) by Jan Vermeer (1632-75), and *Chez Tortoni*, 1878-80 (oil on canvas) by Edouard Manet (1832-83) all courtesy of Isabella Stewart Gardner Museum, Boston, Massachusetts, USA/Bridgeman Art Library. Pages 57 and 58: Illustration of "raining rats" courtesy of NOAA/Photo Library/Department of Commerce. Photographs of Green Toad and Oregon Spotted Frog metamorphosing from a tadpole into an adult courtesy of Suzanne L. Collins, The Center for North American Herpetology. Page 59: Photographs of Vervet monkeys courtesy of National Geographic. Page 60: Photographs illustrating "Dog Talk" courtesy of David Hughes/Hotfoot Studio. Pages 61 and 62: All photographs courtesy of NASA/Chandra X-ray Observatory. Pages 63 and 64: All photographs courtesy of NASA/JPL/Malin Space Science Systems.

DECEMBER 6, 1872 VOLUME XXV NO. 22 PRICE: ONE CENT

GHOST SHIP *MARY CELESTE* FOUND SAILING WITHOUT A CREW

Above: *The* Mary Celeste *sailed smoothly for ten days without guidance.*
Left: *Captain Briggs (pictured), his family, and the crew are all missing.*

PORT OF PORTUGAL – How does a 600-ton (540 t) cargo ship sail 400 miles (640 km) without a crew to steer it or man the sails?

That's the question on everyone's mind today after the *Mary Celeste,* a cargo ship bound for Italy from New York, was found yesterday sailing—unmanned—in the North Atlantic Ocean about halfway between the Azores and the coast of Portugal. None of the ten people supposedly aboard the ship, including seven crewmen, Captain Benjamin Briggs, his wife, and small daughter, has been found.

"It looks like they just disappeared," said Thomas Seaworthy, a British investigator assigned to the case. "There's just no sign of them anywhere, and no indication of what happened. Everything on the ship appears to be in its rightful place—except the crew. They're gone."

According to investigators, the ship was in good condition, ruling out any suspicion of deadly tidal waves or storms. The hull, masts, and sails were all fine, and the cargo barrels of alcohol that the ship was carrying appeared to be untouched. There were no signs of piracy, nor evidence of any illness or epidemic among the crew. "There were no bodies found," Seaworthy said. "If there was violence aboard the *Mary Celeste,* you'd think we'd have found some kind of evidence of a struggle."

According to the captain's log, the last entry was made on November 24, ten days before the *Dei Gratia,* another ship sailing a similar course, discovered the ship. "That means the *Mary Celeste* was at sea for ten whole days without someone sailing her," said Captain Ebenezer DeWitt, who captains a similar-sized ship. "No crew.

(continued on page 2)

IN OTHER NEWS

✦ BOSTON CLEANUP ✦ CONTINUES

Crews continue to assess and clean up the damage from last month's tragic fire in Boston, which destroyed 776 buildings and killed 13 people. See NATION.

✦ NOW BOARDING ✦ TO LOS ANGELES!

California residents can now take a train from Los Angeles to Boston. A wagon ride, the previous method of travel, takes up to six months, while the train takes only six days! See TRAVEL.

✦ BROOKLYN ✦ BRIDGE BOUND

Construction on the Brooklyn Bridge nears quarter completion. Work on the 5,989-foot (1,797m) steel cable suspension bridge that will connect Manhattan and Brooklyn began in 1869 and is scheduled to be finished in 1883. See INNOVATIONS.

THE MYSTERIOUS TIMES ASKED OUR READERS:

What do you think happened to the *Mary Celeste?*

- **58%:** The crew killed the captain and his family then fled
- **22%:** The crew thought the ship was sinking and abandoned ship, only to be lost at sea
- **12%:** Pirates boarded the ship and forced the captain and crew overboard
- **5%:** Space aliens took over the ship
- **3%:** A giant squid or sea creature attacked the ship

(continued from page 1)
No captain. It seems almost impossible for the ship to have sailed so smoothly."

The only thing that suggests the ship may have been abandoned intentionally is the absence of the yawl boat, a four-oared boat used for evacuation. Still, authorities don't understand why anyone would have left the ship with all its valuables, estimated to be worth about $80,000, still on board. "If they were going to abandon ship, you'd think they would take something with them," said William Langley, an Oxford University professor specializing in pirate studies. If the passengers' disappearance was the result of piracy, according to Langley, there would have been some evidence of looting aboard the *Mary Celeste.* "Pirates just don't steal people; they steal goods—gold, alcohol, jewels," Langley said. "I don't think piracy was involved here."

The disappearance of the *Mary Celeste's* crew is the latest in a long list of misfortunes to have afflicted the vessel. The ship was built in 1860 in Nova Scotia. She was originally christened *Amazon* and launched in 1861. Shortly after that, the ship's first skipper, Robert McLellan, fell ill and died.

Shortly after the *Amazon's* maiden voyage, she ran into a fishing weir off Maine and suffering a gash in her hull. Then, after her first Atlantic crossing, she entered the Straits of Dover and collided with a brig, again requiring serious repairs. Upon the *Amazon's* return voyage to North America, she promptly ran aground in Cape Breton Island, Nova Scotia. It was several years later in New York that the ship was re-christened as the *Mary Celeste.*

"I think the ship is cursed," Langley said. "There have been too many misfortunes in a short time for it to be all just coincidence." He added, "I'll tell you this: You couldn't pay me to set foot aboard that vessel."

As investigators continue to search for answers, anyone with information on the crew, the captain, or his family, is urged to call local authorities. ■

DANGERS OF THE SEA

BY PROFESSOR ROCKY C. STORM

While we don't know what happened to the *Mary Celeste, The Mysterious Times* does know some of the perils of trans-Atlantic sailing. Here are just a few of the threats facing ships today:

PIRATES: Robbers on the high seas. Pirates will steal everything from the cargo of the ship to the ship itself. Piracy has been declining since the early 1800s, due to the increased size of ships as well as more frequent patrolling of busy ocean highways, but there are still reports of pirates plaguing the seas.

STORMS: Cyclones, hurricanes, and even very high winds leave ships in danger of damage, capsizing (the boat turning over), or sinking.

ICEBERGS: These floating chunks of ice, of which only one-eighth is visible from the water's surface, can tear holes the bottom of a ship, causing damage that can sink even the largest of ships. Crewmen must always be on the lookout for icebergs, which are found mostly in the colder waters near Antarctica and Greenland.

FIRE: Ironically, this can be one of the greatest dangers aboard a ship, since there may not be enough fresh water to put out a blaze, should one erupt.

SHARKS: Granted, you've got to be in the water for sharks to pose any danger. But if you do jump out of a boat and find yourself floating in the ocean, sharks are something to worry about. Most sharks won't go near people, but some, specifically the Great White and the Tiger sharks, have been known to attack; these sharks are most commonly found in warmer waters.

MARCH 12, 1884 VOLUME XXXVII NO. 5 PRICE: ONE CENT

AMERICA GRIPPED BY LEGEND OF ATLANTIS

"NO REASON NOT TO BELIEVE"

Left: *Ignatius Donnelly, author of* Atlantis. Right: *Plato was the first to write about the city of Atlantis in 355 b.c.*

ST. PAUL, MINNESOTA – It is a city somewhere under the sea where powerful columns rise toward the sky and golden statues shimmer in sparse, water-filtered glimmers of sunlight.

At least that's what former Minnesota Lieutenant Governor Ignatius Donnelly thinks. In his recently released book, *Atlantis: The Antediluvian World*, ("Antediluvian" is a word meaning "ancient") the politician-turned-historian describes the city of Atlantis as a flourishing empire lost to a sudden catastrophe. The story is not a new one. The legend of Atlantis, an advanced civilization on a large island that was supposedly swallowed by the sea after a massive earthquake, has been around for millennia.

The earliest references to Atlantis appeared in 355 B.C. in the writings of the Greek philosopher Plato, who described Atlantis as a utopia, a beautiful island populated by a peaceful people skilled in technology and architecture. Plato said the island was located in the Atlantic Ocean, west of the "Pillars of Hercules," a series of rock formations in what we now call the Strait of Gibraltar.

According to Plato, who described his writings on the lost city as "genuine history," the paradise came to an abrupt end about 9,000 b.c. when a powerful earthquake shook the land. The great empire slid into the depths of the sea, where it supposedly remains today, undiscovered.

But many experts say Atlantis is just a story written by Plato as entertainment. "Nobody's ever found a trace of the supposed Atlantis," said underwater archaeologist Oliver Blue.

"There is no proof it ever existed," agrees archaeologist Ruby Waters. "It's about as believable as stories of giant lizards that once roamed the earth."

Try telling that to Ignatius Donnelly. The longtime politician, who served as lieutenant governor and then congressman from 1859 to 1869, has been researching the so-called "lost continent" for years. Much as

(continued on page 2)

IN OTHER NEWS

✦ FIRST COLLEGE ✦ FOR WOMEN

The United States' first state college for women is established in Columbus, Mississippi. See EDUCATION.

✦ DICTIONARY DOES IT ✦

Twenty-seven years after embarking on a project to create the most complete English language dictionary in history, the first part of the *Oxford English Dictionary* is available. See BOOKS.

✦ STATUE OF LIBERTY ✦ COMING SOON

Construction of the Statue of Liberty is almost finished in France. It will arrive in the U.S. next year. The statue, which will stand on Liberty Island in New York Harbor, will commemorate the alliance of France with the American colonies during the American Revolution. See POLITICS.

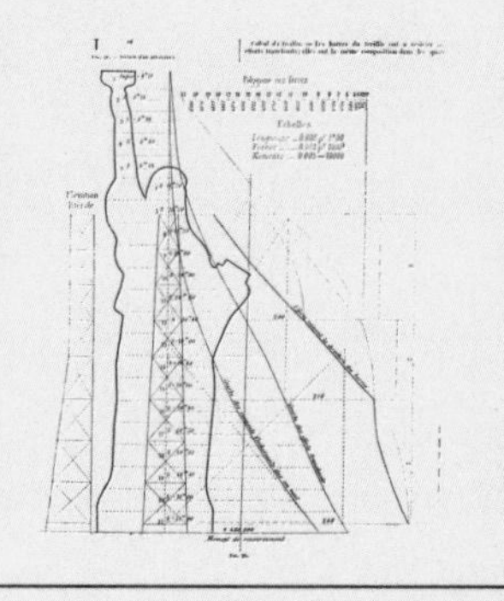

(continued from page 1)
in Plato's writings, Donnelly describes Atlantis as a thriving society with advanced knowledge of technology, whose people live in a city filled with many beautiful buildings. Donnelly also credits the Atlanteans with inventing paper, and says that they were the first to formally study astronomy and to manufacture iron.

"We don't know where he gets his information," Waters said. "Nobody's ever been to Atlantis, seen Atlantis, or met anyone who knows anyone who's from Atlantis."

Despite his lack of scientific evidence, Donnelly's Atlantis talk has drawn many a reader to its mythical gates. Indeed, not since the times of Plato have people been so interested in the myth—or possibly reality—of the sunken empire.

"Who wouldn't want to believe there's a yet-to-be-discovered city out there?" said Roy Smiley, author of the soon-to-be-released book, *Chasing Unicorns: Our Ongoing Search for Unknown Treasures.* "Believing in Atlantis is like believing there's a pot of gold at the end of the rainbow. It's a fun thing to believe."

"I believe in it," said Isabel Wisp, a San Francisco resident. When we asked why, she said simply, "Well, there's just no reason not to believe."

The location of the lost kingdom has been widely debated—everywhere from the icy waters of Antarctica to the sandy desert of the Sahara (some archaeologists say the earth has shifted so much since Atlantis's supposed demise that desert now covers what was once an ocean).

"Wherever Atlantis is, it's left not a trace," said historian Michaeolopolis Flake. "Not in the Sahara desert, not in the Atlantic Ocean, not anywhere. It's a lost city—and a lost cause."

Not so fast, say the believers. Until every sea is scoured and every stone is turned over, they'll keep believing. After all, "There's just no reason not to." ■

Left: *Donnelly's book about a lost land captures readers' imaginations.*

ATLANTIS: WHERE IN THE WORLD IS IT?

In his book, *Atlantis: The Antediluvian World*, Ignatius Donnelly says that Atlantis is located in the Atlantic Ocean, possibly beneath the Azores islands. Plato had placed the lost civilization closer to the "Pillars of Hercules" (now the Strait of Gibraltar).

OTHER POSSIBLE LOCATIONS FOR ATLANTIS INCLUDE:

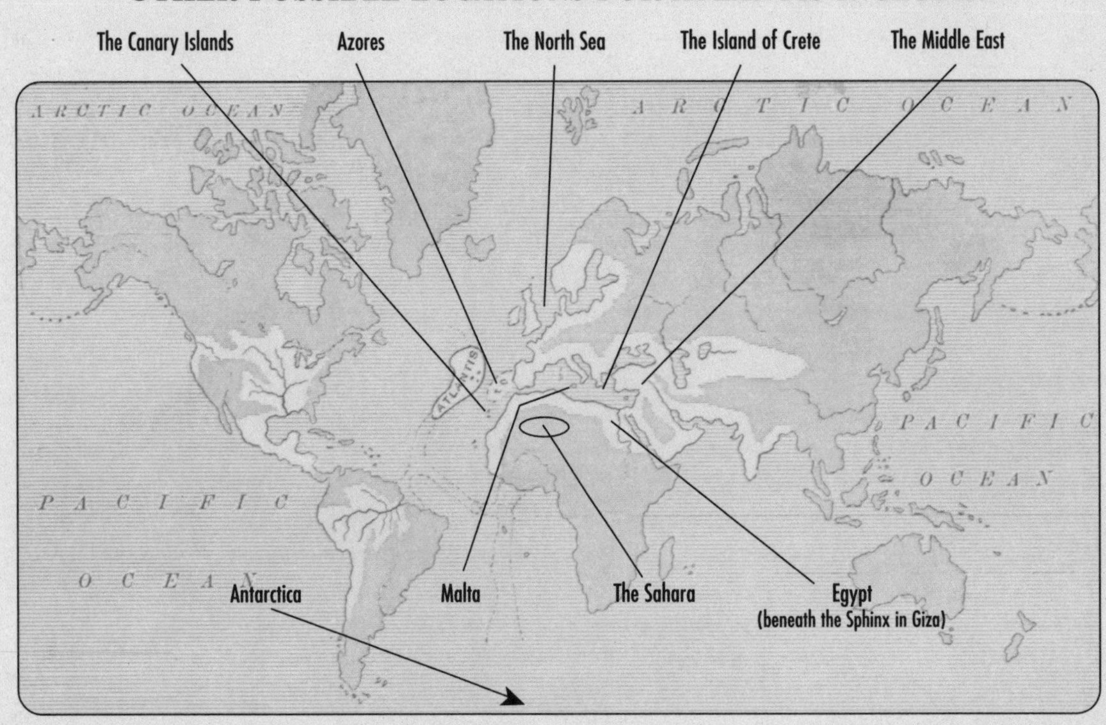

DECEMBER 15, 1905 VOLUME LVII NO. 25 PRICE: TWO CENTS

ONE HUNDRED FORTY ROOMS AND COUNTING

FEAR OF GHOSTS KEEPS WEALTHY WIDOW BUILDING

SAN JOSE, CALIFORNIA – Sarah Winchester already has more than 30 bedrooms, 13 bathrooms, two ballrooms, and five kitchens. What's a few more?

According to *Mysterious Times* sources, Mrs. Winchester, widow of the late William Winchester and sole surviving heiress to the Winchester Repeating Arms Company, said she plans to keep building her San Jose home until the day she dies—even if it's so full of twists and turns that her own servants get lost inside it.

"I don't think even Mrs. Winchester can find her way around this house," said Mr. Jonathan Hammerstein, one of the many carpenters who has worked since 1884 to turn the former eight-room farmhouse into a seven-story labyrinth. "She tells us to build hallways that don't go anywhere, to construct staircases that end at the ceiling. To be honest, I think she's gone mad."

Is she mad? Perhaps. But some believe the reason behind the growth of Mrs. Winchester's far from humble home—which comprises more than 140 rooms, 467 doorways, 40 staircases, dozens of skylights, and thousands of windows—has something to do with the alleged "Winchester Curse."

The curse can be traced back to Mr. Winchester's father, Oliver Winchester, whose company invented the famed Winchester rifle. The rifle, now the most popular gun in the world, was the most advanced weapon made during the Civil War, and was used to kill thousands of soldiers. It was also used against countless Indians during the settlement of the West. It has consequently

Construction of Mrs. Winchester's house continues year-round, 24 hours a day.

become known as the "Gun that Won the West."

Inklings of the curse began when the Winchesters' daughter Annie fell sick and died at six months. Not long after that, Mr. Winchester died of tuberculosis. Stricken with grief, Mrs. Winchester, who was living in Connecticut at the time, sought advice from a medium, a person thought to have the power to communicate with spirits.

The medium informed Mrs. Winchester that the ghosts of all the people killed by her family's rifle were coming back for revenge, and the only way she could escape their wrath was to move to California and start construction on a home

(continued on page 2)

IN OTHER NEWS

✦ FIRST "PIZZERIA" ✦ OPENS IN MANHATTAN

Gennaro Lombardi, who emigrated from Naples, Italy, in 1895, opens a "pizza" restaurant, Lombardi's Coal Oven Pizzeria Napoletana, in New York City. See FOOD AND DRINK.

✦ COFFEE ✦ WITHOUT CAFFEINE?

Ludwig Roselius of Germany invents "decaffeinated" coffee, which offers the same taste without the caffeine. See TRENDS.

✦ THEORY ✦ OF RELATIVITY

Physicist Albert Einstein releases "Theory of Relativity," which dismisses notion that time and space are absolute concepts, suggesting that both can vary with circumstances. SEE SCIENCE.

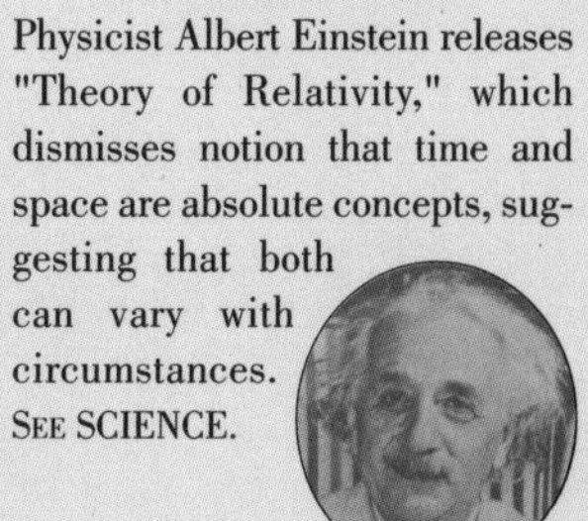

Two of the 140 rooms in the famous Winchester house.

(continued from page 1)

that would never be finished. According to the medium, whose name is not known, ghosts don't like the clatter of construction, so as long as it went on, the enraged ghosts would never settle down.

So in 1884 Mrs. Winchester began to build. And build. And build. And today the building continues—24 hours a day, 365 days a year. Sometimes whole rooms are torn down immediately after they're finished, only to be replaced with new ones.

"The other day, we had just finished a new room exactly the way she wanted it," said Maxwell Cornerstone, another of the many Winchester workers. "She came in, took a look at it, and told us to knock it down and start over! That same day!"

But one thing is clear: Mrs. Winchester, who sketches all the plans herself, is no architect. In-house oddities include a staircase that leads to the ceiling, a door that opens to the floor, and a hallway hidden behind a cabinet. In addition, Mrs. Winchester seems to be obsessed with the number 13: nearly all of the windows have 13 panes of glass, the walls have 13 panels, and almost every staircase has 13 steps. She also allegedly keeps a special "séance room," though none of the Winchester workers were able to comment on this.

"I'll tell you one thing," said Cornerstone. "If Mrs. Winchester has her way, I don't think we're ever going to finish building." ■

THE WINCHESTER HOUSE RUNDOWN (SO FAR)

Stories: 7	**Kitchens: 6**
Basements: 2	**Fireplaces: 47**
Rooms: 140	**Chimneys: 17**
Staircases: 40	**Skylights: 52**
Ballrooms: 2	**Windows: apprx. 10,000**

Can you get out of the WINCHESTER HOUSE?

GET FROM MRS. WINCHESTER'S "SÉANCE ROOM" TO THE FRONT DOOR.

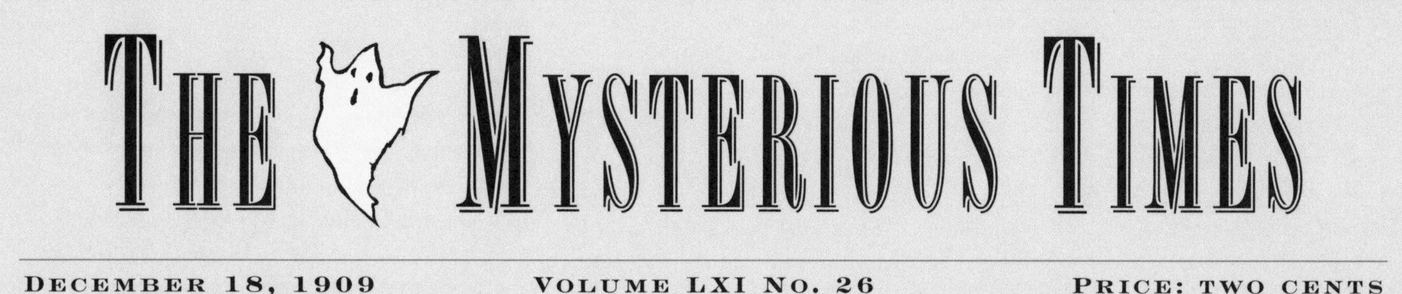

DECEMBER 18, 1909 | VOLUME LXI NO. 26 | PRICE: TWO CENTS

RECENT SIGHTINGS LEAVE PEOPLE WONDERING: *ARE BUTCH AND SUNDANCE ALIVE?*

¡SAN VICENTE, BOLIVIA – "Butch" Cassidy, the notorious bandit who has evaded the law and made off with more than $100,000 robbing trains and banks across the American West, may have been killed last year in a gunfight with local police.

Then again, he may be alive.

Sources say the famous outlaw has been sighted throughout Colorado, Montana, and Utah, the states in which he gained his storied reputation for robbing without ever killing a soul. But the alleged sightings contradict reports that police killed the gangster and his partner in crime, Harry Longabaugh, otherwise known as the "Sundance Kid," last year.

"I wouldn't be surprised if they got away," said Colorado resident Chloë Buttercup. "He's gotten away so many times before."

The name Butch Cassidy is well known throughout the American West—but it is not feared. That's because Butch, who began his life of crime as a teenager, is not the typical criminal. According to records, the infamous bandit, whose real name is Robert Leroy Parker, never killed anyone. He has also been described as friendly, and is known to say "Thank you" at the close of his robberies.

"He's a gentleman," Buttercup said. "One of my friends was at the bank when he robbed it in a few years back. She said he never once said anything vulgar. He even smiled at her and raised his hat as he ran out."

He's certainly spent a lot of time running. But he hasn't always escaped. In 1894 he was arrested for robbing a Wyoming bank. He served 18 months in prison and was paroled, promising never to commit another crime in the state of Wyoming. That didn't stop him. A few months later he was back on a crime spree, getting away with more money than ever.

At some point he partnered with several other bandits, and the gang became known as "The Wild Bunch." Sundance, who would become Butch's right-hand man, was among them.

After eluding the law for more than a decade, Butch and

(continued on page 2)

A WILD BUNCH

The Wild Bunch was formed in the 1890s and robbed banks until around the turn of the century. Despite their "wild" reputation, Butch Cassidy, the leader of the gang, always insisted the bunch commit crimes without hurting anyone. He ordered the bandits to shoot at the horses, not the riders, when being chased by police.

THE GANG INCLUDED THE FOLLOWING MEMBERS:

Robert Leroy Parker – A.K.A. "BUTCH CASSIDY." CASSIDY was the first of 13 children and grew up in Utah. He committed his first major crime at age 22, robbing a Telluride, Colorado, bank of $20,000.

Harry Longabaugh – A.K.A. "THE SUNDANCE KID." Butch's right-hand man and partner in crime. Butch and Sundance left the Wild Bunch in the early 1900s and fled to South America.

(continued on page 2)

(continued from page 1)
Sundance, along with Butch's girlfriend, Etta Place, moved to Buenos Aires, where they continued their crime spree. Etta reportedly dressed as a man during the robberies.

But it all may have ended on November 4, 1908. Or maybe it didn't.

According to reports, a pair of English-speaking bandits robbed a courier near San Vicente, Bolivia. After hiding out in the area for a short while, the two men were apparently killed in a brawl with Bolivian police. The bodies were buried in unmarked graves in a local cemetery. It has never been proven the men were Butch and Sundance.

"A lot of U.S. outlaws like to hide out in South America," said Colorado Deputy Sheriff Yosemite Mudd. "It could have been any one of them."

The only detail that leads authorities to believe the men were the two bandits was the description of their manners. They were called "polite," which fits the notorious pair's reputation. "That's just not enough information for us to say, 'Yeah, they got 'em,'" said Mudd. "I wouldn't believe it unless I saw them for myself."

Consequently, rumors have circulated that the pair, along with Etta Place, have retired somewhere in the American West. "They're probably on a ranch somewhere enjoying their riches," said Utah rancher Wiley L. Buggerbee. "That's what I'd be doing if I was them. Just enjoying the fact that everyone thinks they're gone for good."

If they are caught, Butch and Sundance face severe penalties. Anyone with information is urged to alert authorities immediately. ■

(continued from page 1)

Harvey "Kid Curry" Logan – After a life of crime that began at age 19, Logan was sentenced to 20 years' hard labor at a Tennessee prison but has since escaped. Logan was the wildest of the bunch and the most violent. He is accused of killing at least nine men throughout his criminal career.

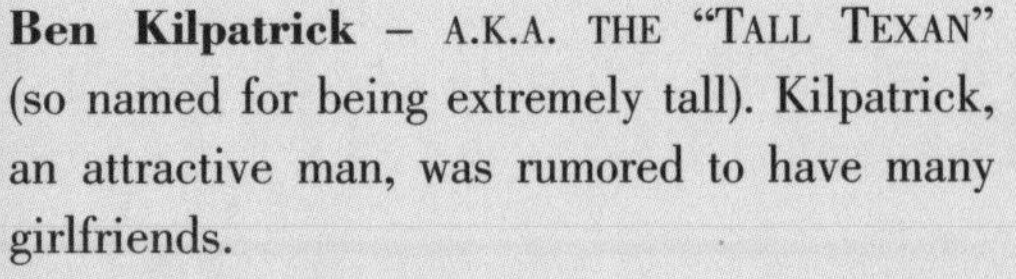

Ben Kilpatrick – A.K.A. THE "TALL TEXAN" (so named for being extremely tall). Kilpatrick, an attractive man, was rumored to have many girlfriends.

Will Carver (DECEASED) – Carver began train-robbing around age 28. He was killed in 1901 in a shootout with police in Texas.

not pictured

Camila "Deaf Charlie" Hanks (DECEASED) – Partly deaf in one ear. He was killed by police in San Antonio, Texas, on April 17, 1902.

THEIR GREATEST TRAIN ROBBERY

On July 3, 1901, the bunch robbed a Great Northern Train near Wagner, Montana, getting away with $65,000.

To pull off the heist, two of the bandits boarded the train, and another one, reportedly Logan, climbed into the engineer's cab with a six-gun in each hand. He ordered the engineer to stop the train. Then, the Sundance Kid and Ben Kilpatrick reportedly ran through the passenger cars, firing their guns at the ceiling and yelling, "Keep your heads inside the car!"

When the train rolled to a stop, Cassidy and Hanks planted a stick of dynamite under the the car and blew off the side. Then they snatched the money from the train's safe.

Rumor has it the gang split up after that robbery, since each member had enough money to live out the rest of his life comfortably.

But robbing trains wasn't always just about money. It was adrenaline that kept Butch and Sundance going, and even after getting away with fortunes, the two kept on robbing.

THE MYSTERIOUS TIMES

OCTOBER 31, 1916 | VOLUME LXVII NO. 20 | PRICE: TWO CENTS

FORMER JOURNALIST DEVOTES LIFE TO SEARCH FOR THE UNKNOWN

Book to Cover Gamut of Oddities

The author, Charles Hoy Fort.

NEW YORK, NEW YORK – Charles Hoy Fort, a former newspaper reporter, novelist, and amateur philosopher, is planning to test the nation's readiness to believe in monsters.

Fort is reportedly working on a book that he says documents a world's worth of so-called "true stories" of strange phenomena, including ghosts, vampires, werewolves, phantom ships, and UFOs.

Ever since he quit his job as a journalist in 1893, Fort has spent his time busily scouring newspapers, magazines, and scientific journals, searching for accounts of anything that "can't be explained," or doesn't fit into current scientific theories.

Working primarily for the New York Public Library and the British Museum, Fort has collected various stories of oddities such as frogs falling from the sky, strange cities appearing in the clouds, and bizarre lights flickering on the horizon.

Reporting isn't new for Fort, who spent a year writing for a New York City newspaper and then worked as an editor for a Long Island paper.

(continued on page 2)

THE STORIES

BY DR. U. WONDER

Fort has devoted his life to the study of strange events and oddities that cannot be explained. "I am a collector of data, and only a collector" says Fort, "but always there is present a feeling of unexplained relations of events that I note, and it is this far-away, haunting, or often taunting, awareness, or suspicion, that keeps me piling on." Some of Fort's most intriguing finds include:

Possible Aliens: In 1843, a worker in a field heard a rumbling sound in the sky, and saw a cloud, under which there were three human forms, perfectly white, sailing though the air above him, not higher than the tree-tops. Fort

(continued on page 2)

Above: *A being from outer space?*

IN OTHER NEWS

✦ WAR RAGES ON ✦

British and French forces are still fighting the Germans in Europe. The war, which began in 1914, is being called history's first "World War," involving nations spanning half the globe. See WORLD NEWS.

✦ VIRGIN ISLANDS TO ✦ BECOME U.S. TERRITORY

The U.S. is planning to buy the Virgin Islands early next year for a price tag of $25 million. Sun and fun aside, the U.S. decided to buy the islands for fear they could be used as a submarine base for the German military during the current war. See POLITICS.

✦ THE AUTOMOBILE: ✦ ALMOST EVERYONE'S GOT ONE

According to recent polls, the automobile has become a common possession among the American middle class. Years ago, it was only the very wealthy who could afford to own one. Auto companies say they hope to make cars accessible to everyone by the next decade. See TRENDS.

(continued from page 1)

"He's a journalist," Van Brain said. "This isn't Edgar Allan Poe we're talking about. He's not telling us about these things because he wants to scare us. He just wants us to know that it's possible there's more out there than we think."

To Fort, nothing is impossible. Consider the case of the strange mirage in the sky on the border of Alaska and the Yukon Territory. It was 1897, and a reporter for London's *Weekly Times and Echo* was quoted as having seen a city within the clouds above the Yukon gold fields. "We were not the only ones who witnessed the spectacle," the reporter wrote. Fort doesn't doubt it.

Fort has also uncovered reports of unexplained appearances, including a story that was published in the *Chatham News* in Kent, England, of a naked man who suddenly appeared on High Street in January, 1914. He ran up and down the street in the freezing cold, until caught by the police. He could explain neither his appearance nor his unclothed condition. Fort noted that despite an exhaustive search, the man's clothes could not be found, and "Nowhere near Chatham was anybody reported missing." Other unexplained appearances included an outbreak of ten "wildmen" who appeared in different parts of England in the winter of 1904 to 1905, one of whom spoke in a language no one at Scotland Yard could identify.

Strange disappearances are equally of interest to Fort, who has collected reports of young men suddenly vanishing without cause, including a series of such incidents in Paris in 1874: "In every case, their relatives and friends declare that they were unaware of any reason for evasion." Similarly, Fort found that "In Montreal, in July and August, 1892, there were so many unaccountable disappearances that, in the newspapers, the headline 'Another Missing Man' became common."

Fort reports the story of "Princess Caraboo, "who, the evening of April 3, 1817, appeared at the door of a cottage, near Bristol, England, and in an unknown language asked for food." Was she a Javanese princess who had been captured by pirates (as one "expert" claimed) or the unfortunate, confused Mary Willocks, lately of Devonshire, who had wandered off, much to her mother's dismay? Fort will not presume to say.

"He's getting the stories, but he's not investigating what's really behind them," said Stone Legend, a scientist who dabbles in paranormal research.

"He's providing a useful service," counters Hannah Spirit, a New Jersey writer. "He's collecting stories of things we cannot explain." ■

MR. DICTIONARY SAYS . . .
Paranormal: Not scientifically explainable; supernatural.

(continued from page 1)

notes that "Unknown, luminous things, or beings, have often been seen, sometimes close to this earth, and sometimes high in the sky. It may be that some of them were living things that occasionally come from somewhere else in our existence, but that others were lights on the vessels of explorers, or voyagers, from somewhere else."

Strange Lights: A "ball of light, or a luminous object" was seen falling from the sky in Burlington, Vermont, in 1907. According to Fort, residents reportedly described hearing a loud explosion, then seeing the strange light in the sky. It was never explained.

Mysterious Creatures: In 1883 the remains of a headless, pig-like animal were discovered on the banks of Brungle Creek, Australia. According to reports, the animal had a tail like a lobster and was said to stretch to about 30 feet (9 m) long. Fort has collected numerous other reports of unknown lake beasts that have attacked and even eaten small animals. However, at least one of these was later found to be an abnormally large fish—though there was no explanation of how the fish got to be so extreme.

Top: *What is this strange light in the sky above Burlington, Vermont?* Bottom: *Rumors of a monster in Lake Washington in Seattle were finally put to rest when the remains of a giant, 11-foot (3.3 m) sturgeon surfaced there.*

THE MYSTERIOUS TIMES

JANUARY 1, 1918 | VOLUME LXX No. 1 | PRICE: TWO CENTS

A TRICK TO TOP ALL TRICKS

HOUDINI MAKES ELEPHANT DISAPPEAR!

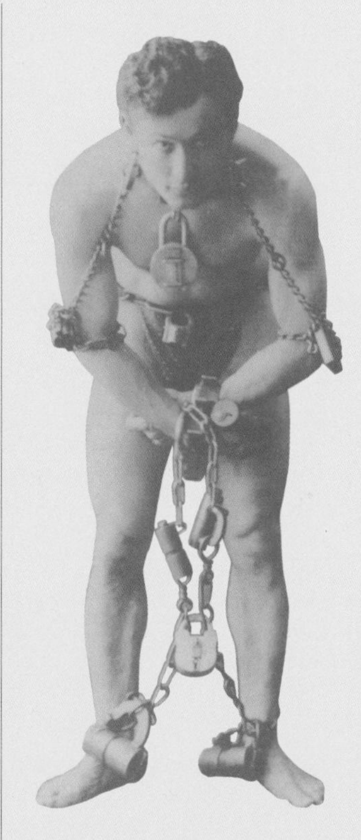

Above left: *In his greatest trick to date, Houdini makes an elephant vanish.* Above right: *Could you escape these shackles? Houdini used his magic know-how to break free.*

NEW YORK, NEW YORK – Master magician Harry Houdini has awed audiences worldwide for more than a decade with his seemingly impossible escapes from shackles, prison bars, and straightjackets.

But nothing could top what Harry did yesterday at the Hippodrome Theater in New York City, when he made a 10,000-pound (4,500 kg) elephant named Jenny vanish into thin air from the middle of a brightly lit stage.

"Pulling a rabbit out of a hat is one thing. Making a couple of doves disappear into a handkerchief—I could do that," said fellow magician Riley Kadabra. "But an elephant? How do you hide an elephant?"

"He just walked Jenny into the arena, fired a pistol, and *Poof!* She was gone," said audience member Billy Mesmer. "I don't know how he did it, but if that's not magic, I don't know what is."

Houdini, like all magicians, refuses to give any clues as to how Jenny vanished. In any case, the "Vanishing Elephant" has made Houdini, a Harlem resident, once again the talk of the entertainment world.

It has not alwys been so; For the young Hungarian immigrant, success was a long time coming. Born Ehrich Weisz on March 24, 1874, in Budapest, Harry arrived in Wisconsin as a toddler when his family emigrated to the United States. They did not thrive financially, and Harry left school at an early age, working as a bootblack and selling newspapers. He became interested in magic after seeing a performance by a traveling magician named Dr. Lynn. At 12, Harry ran away from home; at 16, he became an entertainer.

At first, Houdini did standard card tricks, illusions, and simple box escapes—without much success. In 1896 he almost gave up, running an ad in the newspaper offering all of his magic and secrets for $20. Nobody bought them.

(continued on page 2)

(continued from page 1)

In 1898, he turned to what would become his signature act: the escape. His first escape was called the "Challenge Act," a stunt that finally brought him success. Houdini would escape from any pair of handcuffs the audience could produce. Since then, Houdini has made many escapes. He's escaped from paper bags without tearing the paper. He's gotten out of padded cells, burglar-proof safes, a U.S. mail pouch, a preserved giant squid, and a glass box. "Quite simply, Houdini can escape from anything," Kadabra claims.

"FAILURE MEANS A DROWNING DEATH" blared the ads for Houdini's famous "Milk-Can Escape," in which the magician scrunched himself into a milk can filled with water, unlocked himself from shackles, and escaped within minutes.

Today, the name "Houdini" has become synonymous with "escape." "If a prisoner ever breaks out of the jail cell, we call it a Houdini act," said Stanley Iron, a New York City prison guard. "Thankfully, we don't get too many Houdini acts around here, though."

While it wasn't an escape act, the "Vanishing Elephant" is surely one of Harry's most astonishing feats. "He is always looking for a trick that would make all his others seem easy," Kadabra notes. "His acts just get better and better. What's he going to do now, make all of Manhattan disappear?"

To Houdini, it seems, anything is possible. ■

WHO'S HOUDINI?

Houdini's real name was Ehrich Weisz. He took the stage name Houdini as a tribute to Jean Eugene Robert-Houdin, the most famous magician of the era. "Harry," on the other hand, was simply the American version of "Ehrie," Houdini's boyhood nickname.

BE YOUR OWN MAGICIAN

MYSTERIOUS MESSAGE TRICK

While you probably can't make an elephant disappear, here's a magic trick that you can easily master.

WHAT THE AUDIENCE SEES:

You put a blank piece of paper in an envelope. When you remove the paper, it has writing on it—it's a mystery!

YOU'LL NEED:

- 2 identical envelopes
- 2 identical pieces of paper
- A pen or pencil
- Glue

WHAT YOU DO:

1. Before you do the trick, glue two envelopes together, front to front, so that there is an open flap on each side. (NOTE: DON'T LET ANYONE SEE YOU DO THIS PART!)

2. In one of the envelopes put a piece of paper with writing on it. You can write anything: a secret message, a friend's name, or a fortune.

3. Place the envelopes on a table with the empty envelope flap-side up.

4. When you're ready to do the trick, pick up the blank paper. Show it to your audience. Make a fuss about how it is blank: this is called "misdirection"—everyone's so busy looking at the paper, they don't notice the two-sided envelope.

5. Fold the blank paper exactly as you folded the paper with writing already inside the envelope.

6. Pick up the envelope, being careful to keep the empty side facing your audience. Put the blank paper inside the empty envelope.

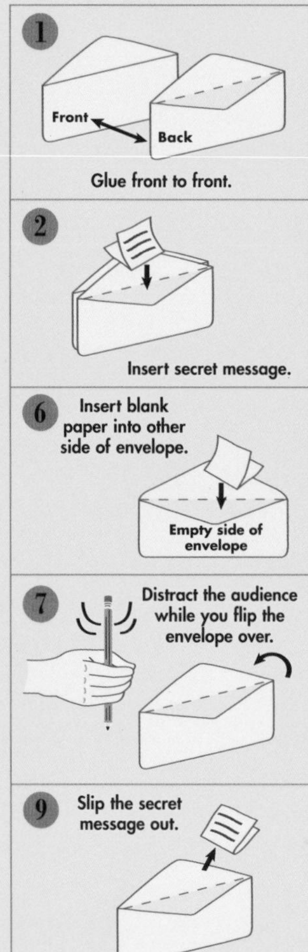

7. Take your pen or pencil and wave it high above your head like a wand, while looking your audience in the eye—this will distract them so they will look in your eyes at or the wand. While you do this, turn the envelope over so that the other side is facing up.

8. Tap the envelope with the pen or pencil, then open the envelope on the side you now have face up.

9. Take out the paper and open it to reveal the message!

10. Everyone will be amazed by your trick. While they are reading the message on the paper, quietly put the envelope in your pocket, so that no one will see the other side.

11. Remember: Never do a trick twice! You don't want your audience to figure it out.

THE MYSTERIOUS TIMES

DECEMBER 17, 1920 | VOLUME LXXII NO. 24 | PRICE: THREE CENTS

MAKING OF STONEHENGE NEAR-IMPOSSIBLE FEAT

Tourists say "Aliens built it!"

LONDON, ENGLAND – Researchers at the University of London say they are discovering more about the origins of Stonehenge, the ancient stone monument in Southwestern England believed to have been created 5,000 years ago. But the biggest questions—who built it and why—remain unanswered.

Earlier this year archaeologists discovered that the massive stones used to build Stonehenge weren't from a local site, but from a mountainous region some 240 miles (384 km) away.

"How does a civilization with virtually no technical capabilities—and this was constructed even before the invention of the wheel—carry dozens of 40-ton (36 t) stones on their shoulders alone?" asks Dr. Phyllis Lugg, a physics professor. "It seems impossible."

Not only did the people who built Stonehenge transport the stones by hand, but they carried them for a very long way. Scientists know this because they recently identified the rock as bluestone, which is found in the Preseli mountains of Pembroke, in Southwestern Wales. The stones are massive, the largest standing about 30 feet (9 m) high and weighing about about 96,000 pounds (43,200 kg).

In order to get the stones from Wales to the Salisbury Plain where they still stand, archaeologists theorize that the builders must have dragged the stones down to the sea, possibly on wooden rollers and sledges, and then loaded them onto rafts. They would have floated along the south coast of Wales and up the rivers Avon and Frome, before being dragged overland again. The final stage of the journey was again by water, before the stones finally made it to Salisbury Plain. Once there, the builders had to shape and raise the stones into position, using only basic tools. The process began about 3,000 B.C. with farmers digging a circular ditch that was probably used in ceremonies and celebrations. Sometime around 2,500 B.C., the first bluestones were brought to the site. About 300 years later, the monument was changed from a relatively

(continued on page 2)

Scientists wonder how an ancient civilization managed to constuct this massive monument.

IN OTHER NEWS

✦ THOUSANDS DEAD ✦ AFTER EARTHQUAKE

A massive earthquake caused a mudslide in Gansu province, China. An estimated 180,000 people are feared dead. See WORLD NEWS.

✦ GETTING AROUND ✦ PROHIBITION

After the U.S. government made it illegal to sell, purchase, or drink alcohol, more and more "speakeasies," illegal underground bars, are cropping up across the country. Speakeasy owners and those caught in them face stiff fines and jail time. See TRENDS.

✦ GO GET YOUR RADIO! ✦

Radios are said to be the entertainment of the future! Regular weekly radio dispatches are expected to be "on the air" by next year. See ENTERTAINMENT.

Stonehenge may have looked like this when it was built.

Stonehenge today.

(continued from page 1)
disorganized formation into an unbroken circle. Then in 1,900 B.C., the bluestones were arranged to form an inner circle and an outer one, the design that still sits in Wiltshire today.

As for the pattern, the perfect circles contain 30 upright stones and 30 stone lintels (the slightly curved horizontal pieces), at the middle of which is a horseshoe arrangement of larger stones, known as trilithons.

"It is a magnificent thing to see," exclaims Harry Jingle, a British tourist. "Something about it just feels magical. It feels like a sacred site."

Sacred? Maybe. Nobody really knows why Stonehenge was built. Some researchers believe it was meant to be a temple for worship of the sun; others think it was an astronomical calculator. It seems the monument was built at least partly to honor and mark the changing seasons. At dawn on the summer and winter solstices (June 21 and December 21), the sun can be seen perfectly framed through the entrance of the monument.

For much of history, Stonehenge has also been linked to supernatural phenomena. In Medieval times it was thought that the monument had been built by giants, or constructed by the mythical wizard Merlin. Later it was thought that extraterrestrials built it as some kind of mapping device.

Scientists today dismiss those explanations as nothing more than fiction. "Stonehenge was built by men—not wizards, or giants, or aliens," affirms Dr. Marianne Marvel, professor of prehistoric studies at a London university. "But why was it built? We still don't know for sure." ■

MR. DICTIONARY SAYS . . .
Stonehenge is called a megalithic structure, which is a prehistoric memorial consisting of a very large stones (megaliths).

A LONG WAY TO LUG!

The path from the Preseli Mountains to the site of Stonehenge is a long one, spanning more than 200 miles (320 km). Archaeologists aren't sure how people carried the heavy rocks all that way but speculate that they used sleds of some sort, and wooden rafts to cross the water.

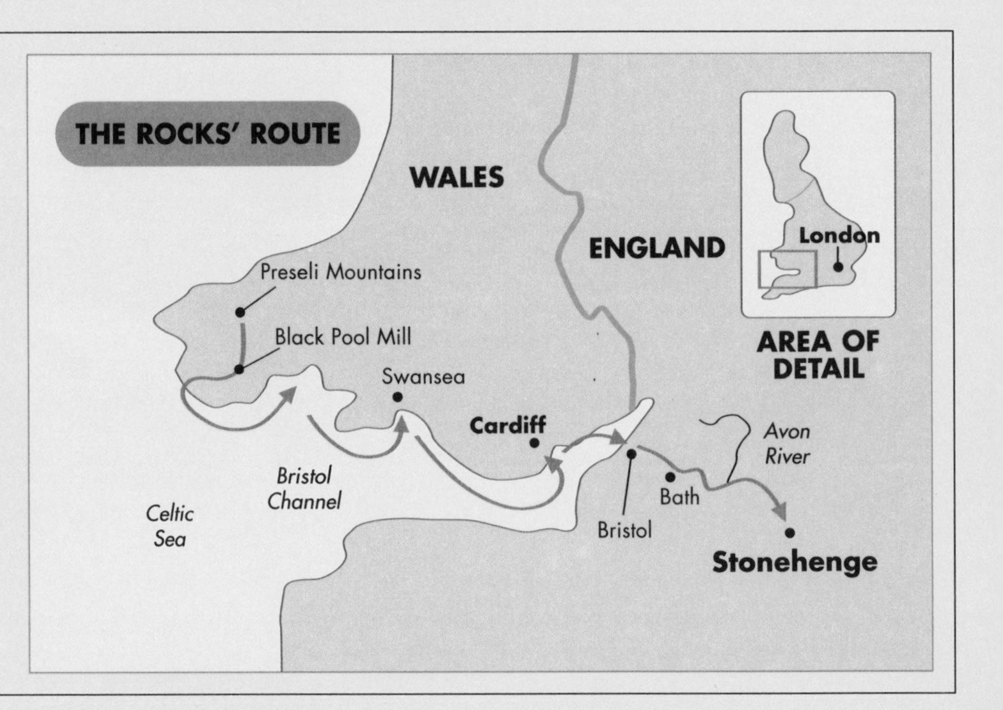

THE MYSTERIOUS TIMES

APRIL 5, 1923 VOLUME LXXV NO. 12 PRICE: THREE CENTS

LEADER OF KING TUT EXCAVATION DIES SUDDENLY: WAS IT THE "CURSE OF THE PHARAOHS"?

Top: *King Tut's golden casket.*
Bottom: *Lord Carnavon.*

CAIRO, EGYPT – People all over the world are fearing the "mummy's curse" after Lord Carnarvon, the man who funded the search for King Tutankhamun's tomb, died suddenly yesterday in Cairo.

According to reports, 57-year-old Carnarvon died from what appeared to be an infection caused by an insect bite. His death came seven weeks after the opening of King Tut's burial chamber and is the latest in a series of strange happenings that have led many to wonder about the supposed curse.

"Death will slay with his wings whoever disturbs the peace of the pharaoh," was the warning excavators allegedly faced when they opened the ancient, treasure-filled tomb of Tutankhamun, the famed pharaoh who died at age 19. It was said the ominous inscription was written in hieroglyphics on a clay tablet, though no such tablet was ever shown to the public.

"It's not clear if there was a warning in the tomb or not," said Gerold Scarab, a historian specializing in Egyptian lore. "But regardless, it is a known fact that the Egyptians took their burials very seriously. They filled their tombs with everything the deceased might need in the afterlife. They believed the dead must remain undisturbed and at peace in order to move into the afterlife. Disturbing the pharaoh would be considered a serious crime."

The young pharaoh's mummified remains lay inside a shimmering golden casket. His tomb, which was filled with golden animals, chariots, statues, thrones, and ornaments, is the only pharaoh's tomb

(continued on page 2)

Treasures found in King Tutankhamun's tomb included golden chests, masks, and a priceless throne.

IN OTHER NEWS

✦ RUNNING ON DIESEL ✦
26 years after Rudolf Diesel invented the diesel engine, the first diesel-engine automobile trip was completed; road trip went from Indianapolis to New York City. See AUTOMOBILES.

✦ A "PENNEY" GOES A LONG WAY ✦
With the opening of a new store in Delaware, J.C. Penney's is now a nationwide chain, with stores in all 48 states.

✦ WHAT'S A "TWINKIE?" ✦
James Dewer of Chicago's Continental Baking Co. invents the "Twinkie," a spongy cake filled with banana cream. Tasters report that the inexpensive treat is delicious.

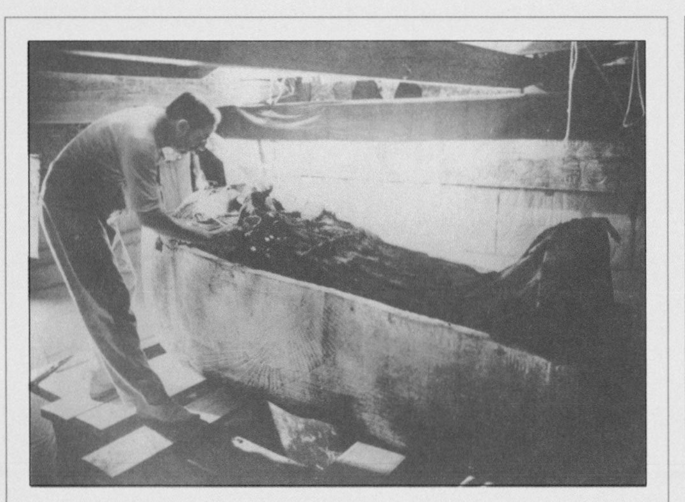

WHAT IS MUMMIFICATION?

WITH EXPERT PROFESSOR WRAPP

The Ancient Egyptians believed that a person would need his or her body in the afterlife. By mummifying a body, they could prevent it from decomposing.

THE PROCESS: First, the internal organs except the heart were removed and steeped in a sodium carbonate solution called natron, which dried them out (the heart was left because the Egyptians believed it was needed in the afterlife). Then the body was filled with natron to dry it out from the inside. After 40 days, the body was washed and covered in oils to help the skin stay elastic. The dried organs were put back into the body, which was filled with sawdust and leaves to make it look lifelike, and finally wrapped in plaster bandages.

(continued from page 1)

archaeologists have yet found intact. Thieves looted all of the others that have been excavated long ago. For unknown reasons, King Tut's tomb lay untouched for nearly 3,000 years.

But last November archaeologist Howard Carter, whose search for the famed mummy was funded by Lord Carnarvon, discovered the tomb. It was buried in the Valley of the Kings, the desolate desert land near the Nile River where many of Egypt's pharaohs were laid to rest. And it was his discovery, some say, which unleashed the curse.

Strangely, on the day the young king's tomb was discovered, a cobra ate Carter's pet canary. In ancient Egypt, cobras were regarded as symbols of the pharaohs.

"The cobra ate the canary because he was hungry," scoffs archaeologist Barbara Relic. "I don't think it was a curse."

There were other oddities associated with the opening of the tomb, however. On the day that Carnarvon died, his dog Susie, who was at Carnarvon's estate in England, was said to have let out a howl and died the exact moment her master passed away. And according to other reports, around the time Carnarvon took his last breath, the lights went out in all of Cairo. The power outage was never explained, though many say the Egyptian electricity grid is prone to outages.

"The media has blown this up to look like something mystical," said Dr. Sandra Goldenground, an American scientist living in Egypt. "There is no curse of the pharaohs. It's all just a story."

But many disagree, saying the events following the excavation are too bizarre to be coincidence.

"It seems awfully strange, no matter how you look at it," said Karen Bumble, an American tourist in Cairo. "I wouldn't want to go near that tomb." ■

MAKE YOUR OWN MUMMY

(NOTE: THIS CAN GET MESSY! BE SURE TO ASK PERMISSION FIRST, AND PROTECT YOUR WORK AREA WITH NEWSPAPERS.)

WHAT YOU'LL NEED:

- Modeling clay or plasticene
- Plaster of paris bandages
- Paint
- Paintbrushes
- Scissors

Making the body:

- Take a lump of clay or plasticene and mush it between your hands until it becomes soft.
- Mold the lump into a mummy's body.
- Fashion a headdress and arms for your mummy (details don't matter; they'll be covered up later anyway). You don't need to shape the legs.
- Add the arms and headdress to the body.
- Cross the arms over the mummy's chest.

Adding the bandages:

- Cut the bandages into strips.
- Dampen the strips in water and wrap your mummy.
- Smooth the plaster with your fingers.
- Throw any away unused materials (but don't throw them down drain).

Painting your mummy:

- You may want to follow a picture (like the one seen on this page) or just use your imagination!
- Paint the headdress first in gold, let it dry, and then apply the black paint over the gold to make the details (like the eyes, mouth, etc.).

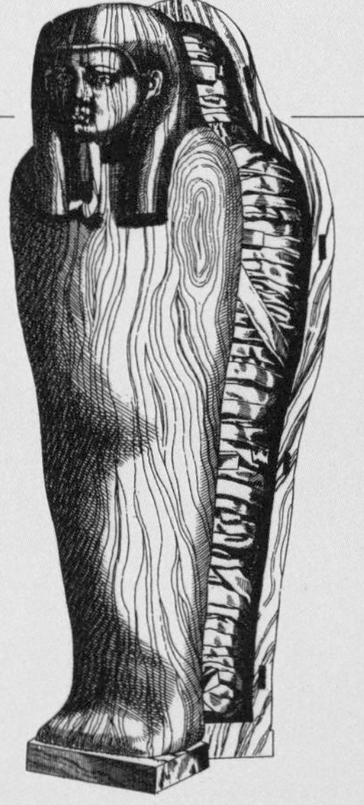

THE MYSTERIOUS TIMES

JULY 18, 1929 | VOLUME LXXXI NO. 27 | PRICE: FOUR CENTS

GREAT PYRAMIDS STILL BEG THE QUESTION: HOW DID THEY DO IT?

PLATEAU OF GIZA, EGYPT – Imagine carrying a 5,500-pound (2,475 kg) rock up a steep hill. Now imagine doing it over and over again for months, then years. It seems impossible. Yet as recent research has found, this is how mere men, using just their hands, built the pyramids of Egypt. It was done without machinery, without pulleys, and without wheels. And it was done 4,000 years ago.

The pyramids are a series of massive burial structures that still stand virtually intact on the plateau of Giza.

How did the builders do it exactly? Archaeologists aren't sure.

"We just don't know," admits Professor Sandy Sifter. "We know they didn't have heavy equipment, obviously. We can only assume that the pyramids were done basically by hand."

Most impressive is The Great Pyramid, which stands 450 feet (135 m) high, and is 756 feet (227 m) long on each side. It is composed of 2,300,000 blocks of stone, each averaging 2½ tons (2.2 t). It was built around 2,540 B.C. to house the tomb of the Pharaoh Khufu.

Above: *The Great Pyramids of Giza: Khufu, Khafre, and Menkaure.*
Left: *Khufu, who was succeeded by his son, Khafre.*

The precision with which the pyramids were created is staggering. The sides of the Great Pyramid face precisely north, south, east, and west. This mathematical accuracy has led to various theorizing about the purpose of the pyramids, including that they were astronomical observatories or alien outposts.

"I don't know about aliens, but to achieve this level of accuracy without technology or machinery is just unbelievable," Sifter says. "We think it probably took about 30 years to build, and involved as many as 30,000 workers. Basically, the greater the tomb, the better the afterlife," he added. To the Egyptians, death was only a journey into another world. The pyramid was its doorway.

The pharaohs were buried with plenty of furniture and riches so as to be comfortable in the afterlife. Servants, wives, and even pets were also often buried close to the king to keep him company.

The thousands of laborers who worked on the pyramids lived in villages that sprang up at the site. Excavations are beginning to reveal the remains of their ancient houses, bakeries, storehouses, and even cemeteries. Some of the workers who built the pyramids inscribed hieroglyphics on the walls of the pyramids as they were building them. Professor Tran S. Lator of the Egyptology Institute explains that this ancient graffiti contains phrases such as "Friends of Khufu," showing that the workers were proud of their efforts on the pharaoh's behalf.

Thanks to the riches that lay within, almost every pyramid was eventually looted by grave robbers. Aside from the

(continued on page 2)

(continued from page 1)

gold-filled tomb of King Tutankhamun, unearthed in 1922, no tomb has since been found with its mummy or treasures intact.

As if anticipating the grave robbers, the ancient Egyptian architects designed passageways that could be sealed with granite, creating hidden rooms and decoy chambers. Consequently, there are some who say perhaps more treasures of the tombs are still hidden somewhere amid the massive stones. But most archaeologists say that's unlikely.

"These tombs contained immeasurable riches," said Katherine Tomes, a graduate student in Egyptian studies. "Thieves would have done anything they could to get at the treasures locked inside. ■

MR. DICTIONARY SAYS . . .
Hieroglyphics: A system of writing made up of pictorial symbols, used by the ancient Egyptians.

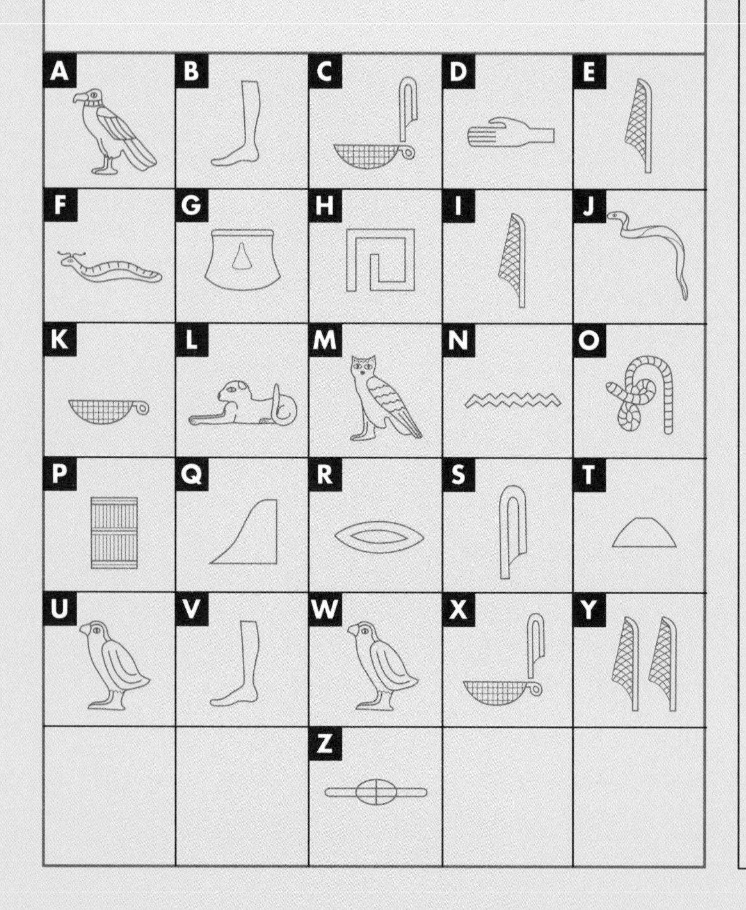

WRITE YOUR NAME IN HIEROGYLPHICS

Try writing your name with this hieroglyphics alphabet.

EGYPT'S NOT THE ONLY PLACE FOR PYRAMIDS

The Pyramids of Giza aren't the only ancient pyramids in the world. Some others include:

Chichen Itza, Mexico: A 75-foot (22.5 m) high pyramid temple built around 1,000 A.D. and dedicated to the feathered Mayan serpent god Kukulkan. The most notable thing about this pyramid is its mathematical precision; the entire pyramid stands as a coded message. There are a total of 365 steps, one for each day of the year. Eighteen terraces represent the number of months in the Mayan calendar.

Angkor, Cambodia: Angkor Wat was built between 1,113 and 1,150 A.D. by the ancient Khmer King Suryavarman II to honor the Hindu god Vishnu. Stretching about one square mile (2.6 sq km) with a series of towers reaching about 213 feet (64 m) high and surrounded by a vast moat, the monument is considered the largest religious structure in the world.

Ancient Babylon: The only pyramid mentioned in the Bible. According to the story, the people built the pyramid in an attempt to climb to heaven. This angered God, and He punished them by confusing their language so they could no longer understand one another. The word "babble," which means to speak nonsense, stems from this story. This pyramid is merely ruins today.

Teotihuacán, Mexico: The name "Teotihuacán" means "The place where men become gods." The complex contains about 600 pyramids of various sizes, built around 100 A.D. Mysteriously, the great civilization that built these pyramids vanished around 700 A.D. To this day, little is known about the disappearance.

The Mysterious Times

JANUARY 16, 1930 VOLUME LXXXII NO. 2 PRICE: FIVE CENTS

CALLING ALL PSYCHICS

DOCTOR DEVELOPS TEST FOR ESP

DURHAM, NORTH CAROLINA Prophets, fortunetellers, mind readers, clairvoyants: Humankind has long had a fascination with the possibility that some people can see into the future. But until now that "second sight" has never been scientifically tested.

Dr. Joseph Banks Rhine, a professor of psychology at Duke University, recently used a special deck of cards to determine whether a person possesses what's called "extrasensory perception," or ESP, which is the ability to be aware of something by means outside your five senses.

"Who hasn't felt like they've known about something before it happens?" said Sue T.H. Sayer, a college student who volunteered for the ESP study. "Or had a bad feeling about something without knowing why. Maybe that's ESP?"

But how do you test something that you just simply "feel"? "Just like you test anything else," says Dr. Wiley G. Wonder, an ESP researcher. "In the laboratory."

To test for the presence of ESP ability, Rhine uses "Zener Cards" (named after the symbols' designer, Dr. Karl Zener), a set of cards consisting of five simple symbols: a star, a plus sign, a circle, a square, and three vertical wavy lines (see illustration, page 2). Five cards of each symbol are used for a total of 25 cards per deck.

Working with his wife and co-researcher, Dr. Louisa E. Rhine, he has developed a scientific method to test for several specific kinds of ESP, including telepathy, which is communication from one mind to another by extrasensory means, and precognition, or knowledge of events before they happen.

In the test for telepathy, the experimenter, called the "sender," shuffles the deck and focuses on each card for a few moments. The test subject, called the "receiver," tries to "sense" the symbol that the sender is focusing on. Each response is recorded, and a correct one is called a "hit."

According to the laws of chance, the average person would generally get one out of five correct, or a total of five hits out of 25; generally, a score of nine hits or more is considered evidence of ESP. Tests are usually done several times on the same subject, just in case a particularly high score is mere luck.

"If a subject gets twelve out of the twenty-five cards, that's considered an example of ESP," Wonder explained. "Most of the time, subjects score a five, six, or seven. That doesn't really mean anything."

Researchers say that while most subjects score unimpressive test results, there have been several documented cases of test-rated ESP.

Still, other scientists are reluctant to accept that ESP exists. Some critics say the test subjects must be literally seeing through the cards, which are made of paper.

"It's got a long way to go until it's accepted by the scientific community," said Dr. S.K.
(continued on page 2)

Dr. J.B. Rhine with co-researcher Dr. Louisa E. Rhine.

(continued from page 1)
Eptic, who has spoken out publicly against the study of ESP. "I personally believe it is wishful thinking."

But many Americans think ESP is a real phenomenon. According to a poll done by *The Mysterious Times*, about 50 percent of Americans believe psychic ability exists.

"I often have dreams about things before they happen," claims Claire Voyant, a New York City resident. "I've thought about old friends and then the very next day run into them at the market. Things like that can't just be coincidence," she added. "Can they?"

Dr. Rhine doesn't think so. He plans to continue applying scientific methods to the study of psychic phenomena in the laboratory in a quest to explain the unexplainable. ■

ARE YOU PSYCHIC?

MAKE YOUR OWN ZENER CARDS TO TEST YOUR PSYCHIC ABILITIES

What you'll need:

Pen and paper • 25 index cards • Scissors • A friend

What to do:

1. Draw the following symbols onto the cards (make five cards for each symbol).

2. Sit across the table from your friend. The person with the cards is the "sender" and the other is the "receiver."

3. The sender should pick up the top card and look at it. Try to "send" the message to the other person's mind.

4. The receiver should try to guess what symbol the "sender" is sending.

5. Write down the receiver's answers. Go through the whole deck, recording all the right and wrong answers.

Scoring: According to the laws of chance, the average person should get approximately one in five right, or as many as 8 out of the 25 cards. A score higher than this may be a sign of telepathic ability.

MR. DICTIONARY SAYS . . .
Extrasensory perception:
Extra = outside of; Sensory = of the senses (sight, sound, smell, touch, and taste); Perception = being aware of.

Try flipping a coin. Can you guess before the coin lands whether it will be heads or tails? If you flip the coin 100 times, the laws of chance say you'll have the right answer about half the time. So if you answer correctly more than 60 times, you might be clairvoyant!

Our Readers React

THE MYSTERIOUS TIMES ASKED OUR READERS: "Do you believe in ESP?"

"I always know when something terrible is going to happen, but no one ever believes me."

—*Cassandra Prophet*,
COLLEGE STUDENT

"When one sense is damaged, another sense often improves, which could be evidence of great undiscovered powers of the mind."

—*T.I. Resius*,
AN ESP RESEARCHER

"I think it's all nonsense. They should study something useful, like accounting."

—*Ima Cynic*,
A DURHAM RESIDENT

The Mysterious Times

SEPTEMBER 15, 1930 | VOLUME LXXXII NO. 19 | PRICE: FIVE CENTS

NEW YORK SUPREME COURT JUSTICE VANISHES

FRIENDS SAY HE LEFT IN A TAXI

Supreme Court Justice Joseph Crater was sworn in earlier this year.

NEW YORK, NEW YORK – It was a warm summer night in New York City when Supreme Court Justice Joseph Force Crater hailed a taxi and vanished without a trace.

It was the night of August 6. The 41-year-old judge and President of the Democratic Pary Club told friends he planned on going to the theater. He hasn't been seen since.

"He just got into a cab and drove away," said Miss Para Legal, who works as a secretary in the New York Supreme Court building. "It's very strange. People like Judge Crater don't usually just disappear. Everybody knew him. It's not like he was a nobody."

Indeed, Crater was a distinguished man in the field of law and politics. Born in Easton, Pennsylvania, in 1889, he graduated from Columbia Law School before opening his office at 120 Broadway, one of the largest office buildings in the world.

In 1920 he was appointed as secretary to State Supreme Court Justice Robert F. Wagner, who went on to become a U.S. senator. Crater also worked as a professor at Fordham and New York University law schools. He was a well-groomed, cultured man, who liked to play the piano, attend the theater, and go dancing. Crater appeared to have everything going for him.

(continued on page 2)

IN OTHER NEWS

✦ JOBS GOING ✦ OUT THE WINDOW

As the Great Depression created by last year's stock market crash drags on, millions of people have lost their jobs, and more and more banks are declaring bankruptcy. See MONEY.

✦ THE DEBATE ✦ OVER SLICED BREAD

It goes stale faster, but it's more convenient. Read what people are saying about Wonder Bread's new pre-sliced bread. See FOOD.

✦ NAZIS ✦ GAINING POWER

The National Socialist Party gained 107 seats in yesterday's elections in Germany. See WORLD NEWS.

(continued from page 1)

"He was a successful, reputable man," said newspaper editor Harvey Scoop. "I can't see what would make him want to disappear from the public eye."

Even Crater's wife, Stella, has no idea where her husband might have gone. The disappearance has left all of New York City scrambling for answers.

"There had to be something going on that people didn't know about," said New York City law clerk Dewey Cheetham. "Something that would make him have to disappear."

Here's what officials do know about the case: According to records, Judge Crater and his wife went to their summerhouse in Maine in June. In mid July he went back to New York to help district leader Martin Healey, who had been accused of selling judgeships, an illegal practice in the court system. On Sunday, August 3, back at the summerhouse, Crater told his wife he was going to New York again for a few days. He reportedly said, "I've got to straighten those fellows out." He said he'd be back for her birthday on August 9.

He never made it back. On the morning of his disappearance, he spent a few hours going through his files. He told his assistant to cash two large checks, totaling $5,150. He took two briefcases of files home and told his assistant to take the rest of the day off. That night, Crater bought a ticket to see *Dancing Partners*, a new Broadway show. Before leaving for the show, he had dinner at Billy Haas' Chophouse with two friends. At about 9 p.m., he hailed a cab. He waved to his friends as he drove away.

Ironically, his disappearance wasn't noticed until several weeks later. When he failed to return to Maine, his wife began to worry. When he missed the opening of the courts at the end of August, his colleagues began to worry. Police were called in on September 3.

Some speculate Judge Crater might have been involved in organized crime, though no evidence has been found to support this theory. Others think perhaps he was having an affair and left town before word got out.

Anyone with information is asked to contact the local authorities. ■

Crater was last seen wearing a brown, double-breasted suit, gray spats, and a high collar, getting a New York City taxi.

WANTED:

SUPREME COURT JUSTICE

In the wake of Judge Crater's disappearance, the New York Supreme Court is seeking a replacement Supreme Court justice. If you are organized, task-oriented, have a law degree, at least six years of trial experience, and consider yourself an ethical person, you may qualify.

Write to:
New York Supreme Court
New York, New York

MISSING

HAVE YOU SEEN THIS MAN?

SUPREME COURT JUSTICE JOSEPH FORCE CRATER

Caucasian male, age 41. Last seen, August 6, 1930, hailing a cab on 5TH Avenue.

Anyone with information please call 555-2000.

APRIL 25, 1934 VOLUME LXXXVI No. 10 PRICE: FIVE CENTS

SOMETHING'S FISHY IN LOCH NESS

TOWNSPEOPLE TALK OF "MONSTER" IN LAKE

"Nessie" is a shy creature; this image of the "Loch Ness Monster" is one of the few existing photographs.

INVERNESS, SCOTLAND – Dinosaurs may have been extinct for billions of years, but according to the people of Inverness, at least one is alive and well in Loch Ness.

Local residents Mr. and Mrs. John Mackay, proprietors of the Drumnadrochit Hotel, were the first to claim a sighting of the creature swimming in Loch Ness, a lake near Inverness. In April of last year, they were driving home from town when they said they saw two black humps drift across the water then sink below the surface. They said it looked like the curved humps of a serpent, or the back of a dinosaur.

The couple didn't publicize their sighting, but word got out, and the story was printed in the *Inverness Courier* two weeks later.

Since then, the "Loch Ness Monster," also nicknamed "Nessie," has been stirring up a lot of commotion in this small Scotland town, with dozens more people reporting sightings of the alleged creature. Residents describe the monster as about 20 feet (6 m) long and dark, probably brown or green, in color.

"We think the creature is a dinosaur that, for whatever reason, hasn't gone extinct," said Margaret McWaters, a nearby resident. "She doesn't seem dangerous though. I think she's a friendly monster."

As for those who don't believe in monsters—or 20th century dinosaurs—Inverness residents say they've seen the photos to prove it. On April 1, Robert Kenneth Wilson of the Royal College of Surgeons used a telephoto lens to snap a picture

(continued on page 2)

IN OTHER NEWS

✦ ALCATRAZ ✦ ISLAND FILLING UP

Prisoners continue to file into Alcatraz, a maximum-security prison located on an island in the San Francisco Bay. Formerly a military fort, the island became a federal prison in January. See LAW ENFORCEMENT.

✦ A NEW MONOPOLY? ✦

Unemployed Pennsylvania salesman Charles B. Darrow has developed a new get-rich-quick game, "Monopoly," based on the promise of fortune. Parker Brothers is said to be releasing the game next year. See BUSINESS.

✦ HOLDUPS CONTINUE ✦

Bonnie and Clyde, the two infamous bank robbers, continue to terrorize the southwestern United States. The pair has been linked to more than a dozen bank robberies and 13 murders, as well as countless store holdups. See CRIME.

(continued from page 1)
of what he claims is the alleged Loch Ness Monster before it sank back into the lake. The photo shows the animal's long neck sticking out of the water like a dinosaur. Or a large log.

"The photo doesn't prove anything," said Timothy Cleary, a biology professor at a nearby university. "That could be a branch or some other debris sitting on the surface of the water. It just isn't clear enough to be substantial evidence."

Some people call the photo proof while others say the search must go on.

"In my mind, there is no such thing as Nessie until I see her swimming around in front of me—not in a photograph, but before my own eyes," Cleary added.

If there is such a thing as the Loch Ness Monster, scientists say it's no wonder the super-serpent chose the murky Loch Ness as its home. At 24 miles (38 km) long, one mile (1.6 km) wide, up to 950 feet (285 m) deep, and with a network of underwater caves and ridges, the lake is a particularly attractive setting for hiding bashful sea monsters.

"You can hardly see your own fishing line beneath this muddy Loch Ness water," said Dougal McDougal, a Loch Ness fisherman. "If there were a sea serpent swimming beneath your boat, you'd probably be the last to know." ■

MONSTER WORD SEARCH

Find the following Loch Ness-related words in this pool of letters:

Loch Ness • Monster • Photo • Lake
Log • Inverness • Scotland

P	T	S	W	J	E	O	L	I	L
R	H	C	R	U	D	R	Z	O	O
I	M	O	N	S	T	E	R	V	C
D	A	T	T	L	A	M	A	U	H
U	A	L	M	O	S	A	T	T	N
R	O	A	R	G	I	S	I	R	E
I	I	N	V	E	R	N	E	S	S
M	U	D	A	G	X	F	U	N	S
T	L	A	K	E	G	O	R	O	C
A	H	E	V	A	C	H	D	O	Y

DO YOU SEE NESSIE?

Loch Ness is a deep, murky lake, filled with mud and underwater caverns and ridges. Even a large monster can hide in these waters. Can you find Nessie living here?

JULY 9, 1937 VOLUME LXXXIX NO. 18 PRICE: FIVE CENTS

EARHART STILL MISSING AFTER ATTEMPTED ROUND-THE-WORLD FLIGHT

COAST GUARD SAYS OUTLOOK NOT GOOD

Left: *Earhart readies herself for what she hoped would be an around-the-world flight.* Right: *Aviator Earhart at the controls.*

HOWLAND ISLAND, SOUTH PACIFIC – In one of the greatest rescue missions ever launched, U.S. Navy and Coast Guard officials are still looking for aviation pilot Amelia Earhart, who disappeared last week somewhere over the Pacific Ocean while attempting to become the first woman to fly around the world.

Navy sources say it's most likely Earhart and her navigator, Fred Noonan, perished at sea, but no pieces of the plane nor any evidence of a crash have been found in seven days of searching.

As a pilot, 39-year-old Earhart is no amateur. She has been flying for almost 20 years and has become the first woman in history to build a celebrated reputation as a successful pilot.

"You could say flying was Amelia's only real aspiration," said California pilot Ely Skybound, who met Earhart in 1922. "She worked harder at becoming a pilot than anyone I know."

Earhart has been dreaming of the skies since her father took her to an air show in 1920. At that time she was 23, and supposedly the minute she saw the planes knew she had to fly. By 1928, she had a pilot's license, her own plane, and a high altitude record. Earhart, one of only about 300 licensed women pilots in the United States, said she was determined to prove that women can do almost anything that men can do.

Indeed, Earhart became a worldwide celebrity and role model for women. Along with her career as a pilot, she was also a contributing editor at *Cosmopolitan* magazine and the president of an all-women flyers' organization called the "Ninety-Nines." "In an age where some men didn't think a woman should drive a horse and buggy, much less drive an automobile, it was a job to prove that females could

(continued on page 2)

IN OTHER NEWS

✦ MAKING ✦ COPYING EASIER

Chester F. Carlson of the U.S.A. is reportedly working on "xerographic reproduction machine," which will be used to make copies of papers and documents. See TECHNOLOGY.

✦ SNOW WHITE: THE ✦ FAIREST OF THEM ALL

Disney's *Snow White* still tops box the office as kids and adults alike flock to theaters to see the film about a beautiful princess, an evil queen, and seven friendly dwarves. See FILM.

✦ JAPANESE ✦ INVADE CHINA

Incident on Marco Polo Bridge leads to war. See WORLD NEWS.

THE MYSTERIOUS TIMES ASKED OUR READERS:

What do you think happened to Amelia Earhart?

- **72%:** Her plane went down in the ocean
- **14%:** She was on a government spy mission and was captured
- **8%:** The plane was shot down
- **6%:** I don't know

They never got there. They were about 20 hours into their flight with about 35 minutes of fuel remaining when Navy radio operators lost contact with them. The last radio transmission put them at about 100 miles (160 km) away from the island.

According to Navy spokesman Ens. Davy Jones, "It doesn't look good. There was no other place for them to land if they were having problems, and they didn't have enough fuel to turn around."

Already conspiracy theories have begun to circulate. Some think the plane was shot down. Rumors have also spread that Amelia was working as a secret agent for the U.S. government and was captured by the Japanese, who have been increasingly aggressive in the Pacific.

Military sources say the most likely answer is the most obvious one.

"They were running out of gas, radio transmissions weren't getting through, and they were tired," Jones said. "The plane must have gone down." ■

(continued from page 1)
fly," said Louise McPhetridge Thaden, a co-founder of the Ninety-Nines. Earhart became a household name in 1932 when she became the first woman to fly the Atlantic Ocean alone.

In 1936, she started planning her around-the-world flight. The flight wouldn't be the first to circle the globe, but it would be the longest, at 29,000 miles (46,400 km) along the equator. She began the historic flight on June 1, 1937, with Noonan as her navigator and sole companion. It was to be a near six-week journey.

The first few weeks went as planned. They made numerous stops in South America, Africa, and Southeast Asia, and had left New Guinea on July 2. At 22,000 miles (35,200 km) into their journey, their next destination was Howland Island, a small island in the Pacific Ocean. It was to be their second-to-last stop before reaching the finish line.

Earhart is always involved in all the preparations for each flight.

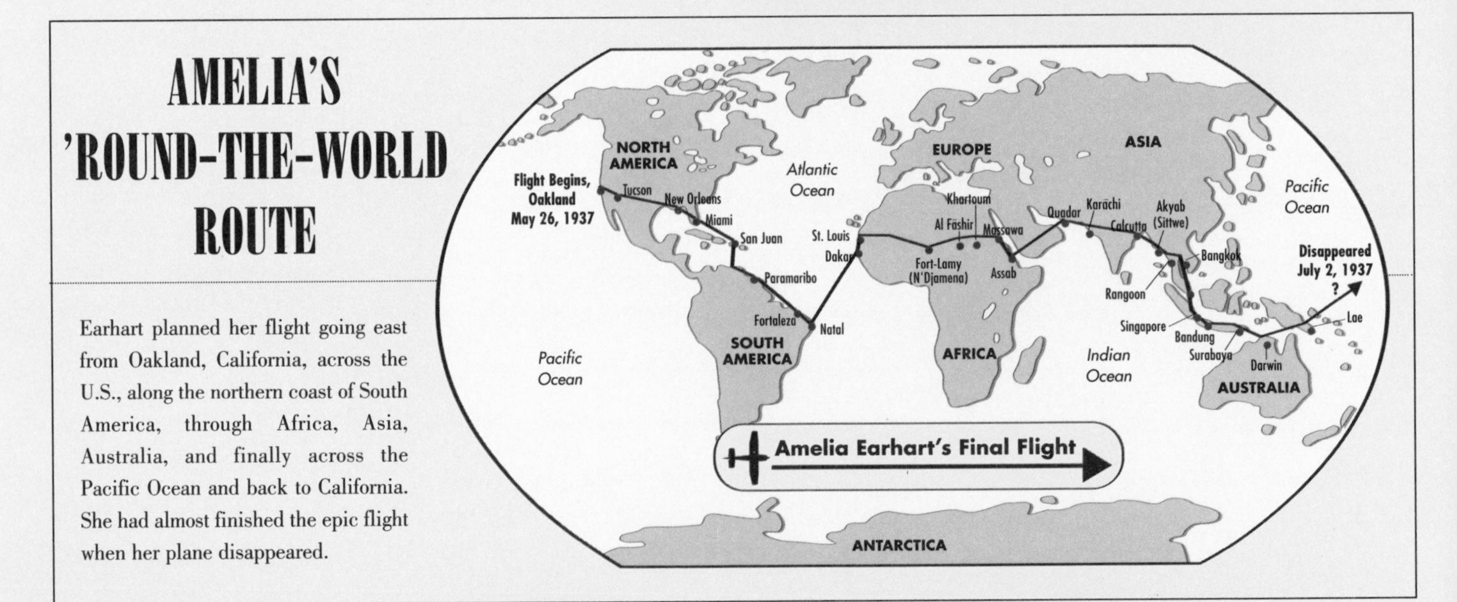

AMELIA'S 'ROUND-THE-WORLD ROUTE

Earhart planned her flight going east from Oakland, California, across the U.S., along the northern coast of South America, through Africa, Asia, Australia, and finally across the Pacific Ocean and back to California. She had almost finished the epic flight when her plane disappeared.

THE MYSTERIOUS TIMES

December 5, 1940 | Volume XCII No. 21 | Price: Six cents

LOST COLONY OF ROANOKE STILL LOST

"CLUES" TURN OUT TO BE HOAX

An artist's interpretation of the lost settlement on Roanoke Island, North Carolina.

ROANOKE ISLAND, NORTH CAROLINA – A series of stones found scattered in a Roanoke Island swamp and thought to be clues left behind by a colony that seemingly vanished in the late 16th century have turned out to be nothing more than a hoax.

When the stones were first found, etched with puzzling letters and words, it was thought they were 350-year-old messages from Eleanor Dare, one of about 112 colonists who sailed from England to Roanoke Island in 1587. They were the first English colony in North America, a brave group of men, women, and children.

But three years after they arrived on the island, which is situated off the coast of Virginia, the colonists were discovered missing. Historians have guessed at their fate and archaeologists have searched for their remains, but nothing has ever been found. Until the carved stones.

The stones were engraved with a message, believed to be from Eleanor, explaining that the settlers had fled the island after a Native American Indian attack. But a journalist recently proved that the carvings were planted by locals who wanted to mislead eager historians.

"We thought it was the missing link, the key to figuring out how 112 people could have disappeared without a trace," said historian Pratt C. Prior. "But now we're back to where we started."

What historians do know is that in 1587, John White disembarked onto the shores of Roanoke Island with a colony from England. White's daughter, Eleanor Dare, and soon-to-be-born granddaughter, were among the colonists.

At the time, Roanoke Island was thought to be a perfect settlement. It was a land rich with

(continued on page 2)

Three years after the colony was settled, the residents all vanished, leaving behind few clues.

IN OTHER NEWS

✦ OPEN ROAD IN CALIFORNIA ✦

California is gearing up to open its first freeway, the Arroyo Seco Parkway, in Los Angeles. See TRANSPORTATION.

✦ HOW GOOD IS "KENTUCKY FRIED CHICKEN"? ✦

Mysterious Times food critic Benjamin Yum reviews Colonel Sanders's new recipe for "Kentucky Fried Chicken." Sanders developed the recipe this year and plans on selling the tasty concoction all over the country. See FOOD.

✦ BRITAIN UNDER SIEGE ✦

Sirens wail nightly as Luftwaffe planes continue to rain destruction on Britain. See WORLD NEWS.

The word "Croatoan," the name of a nearby Native American village, is one of the few clues the settlers left behind.

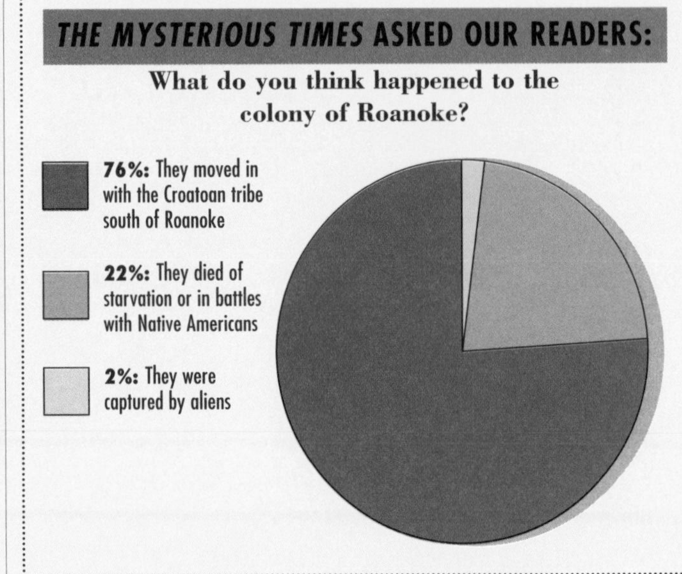

(continued from page 1)

fruit and wildlife and had a relatively warm climate year round. The Native American Indians were friendly initially, sharing their food and trading their wares with the settlers.

Shortly after the birth of his granddaughter, White left the colony, promising to return within the year with more food and supplies. But a war between England and Spain broke out in the interim, and he was not able to return until three years later.

By then the settlers were gone. The only things left in their wake were two strange carvings: one, etched on a post, read "CROATOAN"; the other, on a nearby tree, read "CRO."

Croatoan was the name of a Native American village on an island several miles south of Roanoke. Had the settlers gone there? "They were friendly with the Native Americans," said historian Francis Byron Jake. "They depended on them for food since they hadn't yet learned how to farm the land."

"We assume that's what happened," Prior said. "But why didn't they leave more information? And why were they in such a hurry that they couldn't finish the second carving?"

White tried to sail to Croatoan, but a violent storm prevented him from going south. Reluctantly he returned to England.

The settlers' bodies were never found and not one of them ever surfaced to tell their side of the story.

Of the recently discovered stones, Jake added, "We had hoped those stones would have been our storyteller. But now the lost colony of Roanoke is as lost as ever." ■

MAP OF THE ROANOKE COLONY

This map shows the location of the long-lost Roanoke Island settlement.

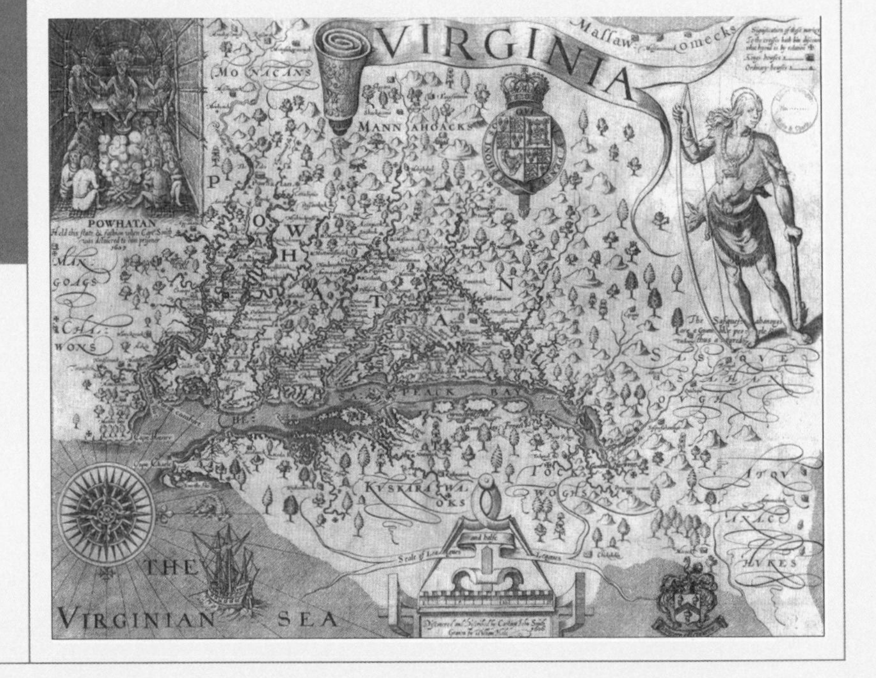

THE MYSTERIOUS TIMES

December 6, 1945 | Volume XCVII No. 51 | Price: 10 cents

NAVY PLANES DISAPPEAR OFF COAST OF FLORIDA

IS "BERMUDA TRIANGLE" TO BLAME?

Above left: *Navy fighter jets like those that vanished off the coast of Florida.*
Above right: *Approximate location of the so-called "Bermuda Triangle."*

FORT LAUDERDALE, FLORDA–In the latest in a long list of strange disappearances in the waters off the coast of Florida, five U.S. Navy fighter planes vanished without a trace yesterday after taking off on a routine training mission. None of the men aboard have yet been found.

According to *Mysterious Times* sources, the five torpedo bombers lifted into sunny skies from the U.S. Naval Air Station in Fort Lauderdale, led by instructor Lieutenant Charles Taylor. The training mission, known as Flight 19, was to carry out a few practice runs and then return to the base.

"It was a standard mission," said Navy spokesman Lt. Jerry Stronghold. "Lt. Taylor had done it before. It should have been a quick, roundabout mission."

Transcripts of communications between Taylor and the base suggest that Taylor's compass may have been malfunctioning, but there has been no explanation for why the compass should have failed.

Since the disappearance, Navy pilots have been flying over Flight 19's path, but nothing has been found to indicate where the planes went down—or even if they went down.

"We've scoured the area," Lt. Stronghold said. "If those planes went down, you'd think we would have recovered a few scraps of debris. But we've found nothing."

Meteorologists have indicated bad weather could have caused problems for the pilots. Reports of a storm brewing off the eastern coast of Florida have led investigators to condsider the possibility of strong winds,

(continued on page 2)

IN OTHER NEWS

✦ U.S. JOINS ✦
UNITED NATIONS

By a vote of 65 to 7, the U.S. Senate approved the United States' participation in the international organization called the United Nations. The first general assembly, made up of 51 nations, will not be held until January. See WORLD NEWS.

✦ "COMPUTER" MAKES ✦
FIRST CALCULATIONS

The "Electronic Numerical Integrator and Computer," which covers 1,800 feet (540 m) of floor space, is still undergoing tests. Last month, the computer made its first set of calculations. See TECHNOLOGY.

✦ EVERYONE WANTS ✦
A SLINKY!

U.S. Navy engineer Richard James manufactures the "Slinky," a metal-spring toy that appears to "slink" itself down stairs. James said he invented the toy, which is already disappearing from toy store shelves, by accident. See LEISURE.

(continued from page 1)
rain, and lightning as factors in the disappearance. Navy meteorologist Skipper Storm noted, "It could have been very tough flying."

"But still," he added, "it is unusual for all five planes to have completely disappeared."

But it's not the first time that strange events have occured in these waters. The area—a triangular region bound by Bermuda, Puerto Rico, and Florida—has been at the center of several unexplained disappearances and peculiar maritime phenomena for hundreds of years.

It was Christopher Columbus who first reported odd happenings in the region. In 1492, as the explorer sailed through the triangle on his way to the New World, he reported compass malfunctions and strange lights in the sky along the horizon.

To date, dozens of ships and a handful of planes have disappeared in the area, including the U.S.S. *Cyclops*, which vanished in 1918 with 309 crewmen aboard, and earlier this year, a Martin Mariner training aircraft with 12 crewmen—not to mention numerous civilian vessels. Navy officials insist nothing out of the ordinary is at work, saying that it's not uncommon for ships or planes to malfunction en route.

Scientists say the region, also known as the "Devil's Triangle," is one of the few places on Earth where a magnetic compass points toward true north. Normally a compass points toward the magnetic north, which is different by about 20 degrees.

"This small variation might be what's causing ships and planes to lose their way," said navigational expert Halpern West.

Lacking any debris from the lost planes, it may never be clear what happened. And left without hard answers, many people are looking to the supernatural to explain the planes' disappearance.

"I think they got scooped up and whisked away to another world," says Gerard Gist, a Florida fisherman. "I think that's what happened to all those others."

"Maybe they flew straight on into the past," wonders Florida resident Virginia Biddel. "I guess we'll never know." ■

BERMUDA TRIANGLE DISAPPEARANCES:

A Short List of Missing Ships and Crews

1609	The *Sea Venture* and its rescue boat disappeared just off Bermuda's coast.
1840	The *Rosalie,* a French vessel, was found derelict—cargo intact, crew missing.
1880	The *Atlanta,* a British frigate, disappeared near Bermuda with 290 passengers onboard.
1902	The *Freya,* a German bark, was discovered crewless soon after leaving Cuba; the ship was listing badly and partly dismasted.
1924	The *Raifucu Maru,* a Japanese freighter, radioed for help but was never found.
1932	The *John and Mary* was found abandoned south of Bermuda, sails still furled, hull freshly painted.
1944	The *Rubicon,* a Cuban freighter, was discovered without its crew; only a dog remained onboard.

Our Readers React

THE MYSTERIOUS TIMES ASKED OUR READERS:

"What do you think happened to Flight 19?"

"I think it was aliens. I think those planes were zapped outta the sky by extraterrestrials. You know, from some other planet. I bet they were green and flew in spaceships that made loud buzzing sounds. That's what I think."

—Timothy Jinglemeyer, 11,
FIFTH GRADER

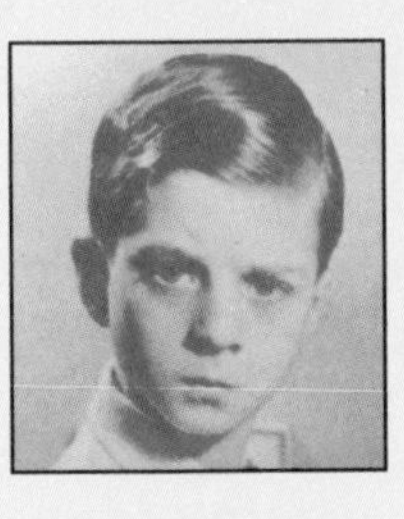

"It was probably a simple explanation. Probably just bad weather—you know, thunder and lightning or something like that. Planes go down all the time. It's nothing that extraordinary."

—Arthur Bundlestiff, 45,
ATTORNEY

"Maybe they were pulled into another dimension, another time. Maybe, somehow, they flew their planes right into the age of the dinosaurs. You never know."

—Buttercup Fauna, 31,
FLORIST

"I think they flew the planes on a secret mission and they're just not telling us about it. The Navy knows. They're probably on some spy mission, and we'll never know what happened to them. Top secret stuff, ya know?"

—Mugsy Muddzino, 35,
BOXER

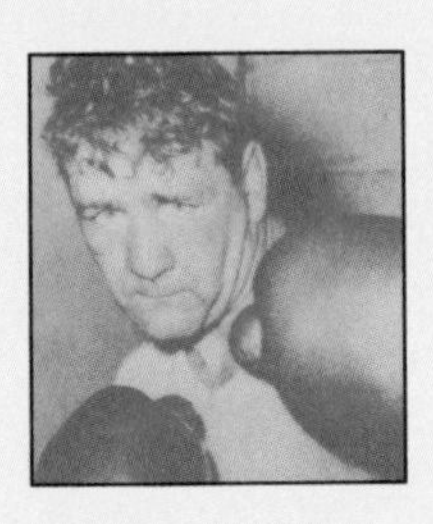

THE MYSTERIOUS TIMES

July 10, 1947 | Volume C No. 29 | Price: 10 cents

GOVERNMENT DENIES FLYING SAUCER CLAIM:

ROSWELL RESIDENTS NOT SO SURE

ROSWELL, NEW MEXICO – Two days ago, the *Roswell Daily Record* published news of a "flying saucer" found on a New Mexico ranch. The July 8 headline blared "ROSWELL ARMY AIR FIELD CAPTURES FLYING SAUCER." The story reported that the Intelligence Officer of the 509th Bomb Group, stationed at Roswell AAF, had recovered a "flying disc" from the range lands of a local rancher; in the same story it was noted that a Roswell couple claimed to have seen a large unidentified object fly by their home earlier in the week.

After the story was picked up by newspapers and television stations around the globe, it now appears the media may have jumped the gun. According to government sources, the metal debris found on a Roswell ranch—the so-called flying saucer—was a harmless high-altitude weather balloon, the kind, military officials say, that is used to measure wind currents.

Local rancher W.W. Brazel found the debris about eight miles (13 km) from his ranch, which is 85 miles (136 km) northwest of Roswell. He described it to reporters as a scattering of rubber strips and what looked like scraps of torn tinfoil. At the time he said he thought nothing of it.

It was only after he went to town and heard stories about other people having seen unidentified flying objects that he realized that may have been what crashed into the desert landscape of his ranch. He quickly told Roswell Sheriff George Wilcox about the finding.

Wilcox called Major Jesse A. Marcel of the Roswell Army Air Field, who promptly came and picked up the debris.

By the end of the day, the Air Force had denounced the finding as insignificant, but it was *(continued on page 2)*

Above left: *Roswell, New Mexico.* Above right: *Evidence of a crashed spaceship?* Below: *Walker Airforce Base, Roswell, NM.*

(continued from page 1)
too late; the local press had already run the story about the alleged "flying disk."

According to reports, respected Roswell residents Mr. and Mrs. Dan Wilmot said they saw the flying disk for themselves. They told the *Roswell Daily Record* that they watched an object, which appeared to be about five feet (1.5 m) in height and 15 to 20 feet (4.5-6 m) in diameter, streak across the sky for about 45 seconds before disappearing over the distant hills.

Reports of bodies found at the sight have been dismissed by officials: "Those were anthropomorphic dummies used for scientific tests," said a military spokesman, "just big dolls, not aliens."

The excitement over supposed UFO sightings is nothing new. Just two weeks ago, a pilot named Kenneth Arnold reported seeing several objects in the sky near Mt. Rainier, Washington. He described the objects as "geese" that moved like saucers skipping across the water. Thus the term "flying saucer" was born.

Military sources deny that what Arnold saw in the sky that night was anything otherworldly. "We're not opposed to finding a UFO," said Army Sergeant Dapper Strongarm. "We simply haven't seen any real evidence. These are all just stories people tell."

Rumors persist, however, that the shreds of metal found in Roswell, are not of human manufacture. "It's a cover-up," said May B. Allien, publisher of *UFO TODAY,* a newsletter that chronicles unexplained flying objects. "The military wants to keep the spacemen's technology for itself. But we know they're out there, and we'll keep searching for the truth." Allien and her supporters are offering a reward of $3,000 to anyone who can provide physical evidence of the extraterrestrials.

MAKE YOUR OWN ALIEN ANTENNAE

Nobody knows for sure what aliens look like, but many people think they may have long antennae, like bugs. Try this craft project to make your own pair. They're easy to make and fun to wear!

What you'll need:

Pipe cleaners • Small styrofoam balls
Colored markers • Headband

Directions:

- Decorate the Styrofoam balls any way you'd like. (Draw silly designs or make them all one color—be creative!)
- Wrap the bottoms of two pipe cleaners twice around the headband so about 6 to 8 inches (15-20 cm) of each pipe cleaner sticks up securely from headband.
- Fasten the Styrofoam balls onto the ends of the pipe cleaners.

MR. DICTIONARY SAYS . . .
Ufology= The study of unidentified flying objects.

★ ★ ★ IS IT A UFO? ★ ★ ★

Roswell isn't the only place where UFOs have been suspected to roam the skies. Americans have been reporting "flying saucers" all over the country. But almost all of these reports have turned out to be nothing otherworldly. The following are some items that could look like a spaceship in the sky.

Bird (blacked out by the sun) • **Balloon**
Weather balloon • **Plane**

THE MYSTERIOUS TIMES

November 11, 1956 | Volume CIX No. 45 | Price: 15 cents

CONSPIRACY THEORIES ABOUND

IS AREA 51 HIDING PLACE FOR ALIEN SPACECRAFT?

Top: *The military base known as "Area 51".* Bottom: *Alleged U.F.O. sighting above Area 51.*

GROOM LAKE, NEVADA – Almost 10 years after a weather balloon thought to be a UFO crashed in Roswell, New Mexico, spreading suspicion that the government was hiding information about extraterrestrials, it now appears that a top secret military installation may be sparking the same out-of-this-world notions.

The military base, a stretch of Nevada desert about 90 miles (144 km) north of Las Vegas, is also known as "Area 51." Government officials claim it is a testing site. Others claim it's much more.

"They're hiding things inside that facility," claims Ufologist Harvey Moonwalker, Ph.D. "There's just too much secrecy, too many 'Keep Out' signs. There's something they're not telling us."

Moonwalker and his colleagues believe the government is using Area 51 to store crashed alien spacecraft, possibly to develop new, alien-inspired technology.

"Nonsense," says the government. While officials admit to Area 51's secrecy—the entire region is strictly confidential and off-limits to civilians—they firmly deny any connection with aliens.

Protected by about 1,000 miles (1,600 km) of restricted airspace and surrounded by sprawling empty desert, the Groom Lake base, which opened in 1954, has so far been used for testing advanced aircraft. According to a *Mysterious Times* source, the government uses the base to test its new U-2 spy plane. Groom Lake's remoteness makes it an ideal place for flight tests, and more are expected in the future. In fact, construction began this year on a 5,000-foot (1,500 m) runway to be added to the facility.

In addition to testing warplanes, Area 51 is far enough *(continued on page 2)*

IN OTHER NEWS

✦ WIN BIG ON TV! ✦

Our television critic reviews "The Price is Right," a new NBC television game show that offers contestants the chance to bid on fabulous prizes. See TELEVISION.

✦ DESTINATION: DISNEY ✦

Crowds continue to rush to Disneyland, a theme park in Anaheim, California, based on the characters of Walt Disney films. Travel experts say the park, which opened last year, is quickly becoming one of America's most-visited destinations. See TRAVEL.

✦ AMERICA LOVES POTATOES! ✦

"Mr. Potato Head" delights children of all ages. The toy is made up of plastic face parts that kids can stick into real potatoes to form funny faces. Toy manufacturers say the toy will soon come with a plastic potato body, which will replace the need for a real potato. See TOYS AND GAMES.

(continued from page 1)
away from any residential area to allow for military weapons testing that may otherwise threaten local communities. Officials would not say what kind of weapons may be tested at the base but will say they have nothing whatsoever to do with extraterrestrial technology.

"I can assure you, there's nothing strange going on here," said a military official who refused to be identified. "Area 51 is not hiding aliens, or alien ships, or anything having to do with aliens."

But residents who live in the area think otherwise. Some say they have seen strange lights in the sky near the base, lights moving in ways that modern aircraft can't—darting up and down and diagonally across the sky. A few people claim to have seen an actual spaceship being lugged into the facility.

"I don't know what to believe," said Las Vegas resident Sam Mulder. "I've heard of strange goings-on, but when I tried to check it out, I couldn't get close enough to the place to see anything."

Moonwalker has collected numerous verbal reports of glowing orbs seen above the Groom Lake installation, and rejects the government's explanations. "We know they are testing stuff in there that's just too technologically advanced to have originated here on Earth," he charged. "Workers at the facility, who are too frightened to speak publicly, have told us of metals that don't melt even when exposed to high temperatures, and a kind of so-called 'cloaking technology' that would allow planes to fly undetected—almost as if they were invisible. There's no way our military could have developed that stuff without help from a more advanced society."

A spokesman for the facility said only, "No comment." *The Mysterious Times* says, "Time will tell." ■

U.F.O. GALLERY:

HERE ARE A FEW UFO PHOTOS SENT IN BY *MYSTERIOUS TIMES* READERS. WHAT DO THEY LOOK LIKE TO YOU?

Our Readers React

THE *MYSTERIOUS TIMES* ASKED OUR READERS:

"Is there alien spacecraft hidden in Area 51?"

"I don't think there are any strange things going on. If they're making weapons, testing planes, that's their right. They're the military. But do I think they're dissecting aliens? What are you, crazy?"

—*Gilfred Wiseman, 43,*
AUTO MECHANIC

"It does seem awfully odd that they have to make that whole area so secret. But I don't know if there's anything alien going on there. That's a stretch, I think."

—*Winnie Telebuzz, 28,*
BEAUTICIAN

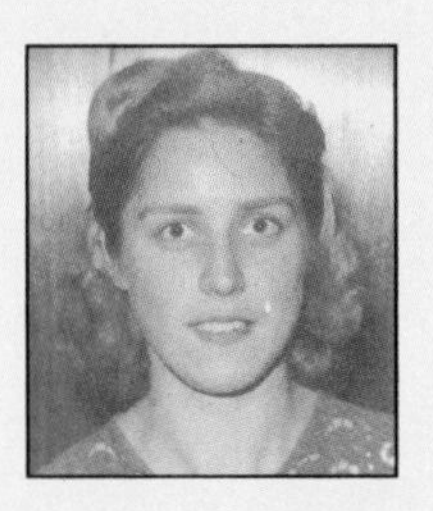

"You read about that spaceship landing in Roswell? I bet it's down there. I'd like to meet the spacemen—could you give them my number?"

—*Vixen Lemore, 23,*
WAITRESS

THE MYSTERIOUS TIMES

June 13, 1962 | **Volume CXV No. 26** | **Price: 20 cents**

ESCAPE FROM ALCATRAZ!

SEARCH IS ON FOR THREE MISSING PRISONERS

SAN FRANCISCO, CALIFORNIA– Despite a massive land, water, and air search, law enforcement officials have so far been unable to find the three prisoners who were discovered missing from their cells yesterday morning.

According to the FBI, it appears the convicts, all three of whom were serving time for bank robbery, broke out of the famed high-security prison by digging holes through the walls and escaping through a network of tunnels and ventilators.

The men apparently used spoons stolen from the prison cafeteria as small shovels to chip away at the eight-inch (20 cm) concrete walls.

"It must have taken months for them to dig their way out," said prison guard Jeremiah Bars. "And with spoons? It's just astounding."

The men were identified as Frank Lee Morris, 35, a robber from Louisiana; John W. Anglin, 32, and Clarence Anglin, 31, two of three Florida brothers imprisoned for an Alabama bank robbery. Morris, who is reportedly extremely intelligent with an IQ of 133, appears to have organized the breakout.

For more than a quarter century, Alcatraz has been hailed as one of the most secure prisons in the country and has housed such legendary prisoners as Al Capone. It sits, isolated, in the middle of the San Francisco Bay about a mile (1.6 km) from the shore and surrounded by cold waters with strong currents.

In its 28 years of operation, 31 men (not including this latest escape) have attempted to escape Alcatraz. All of them were either caught, shot, or drowned in the bay.

The prison's latest escapees were discovered missing Tuesday morning when they failed to appear for the morning roll call. Officers assumed the men were still sleeping and *(continued on page 2)*

Above: *Alcatraz Island is situated in the bay off San Francisco.*
Below: *The escapees fooled guards by placing dummies in their beds.*

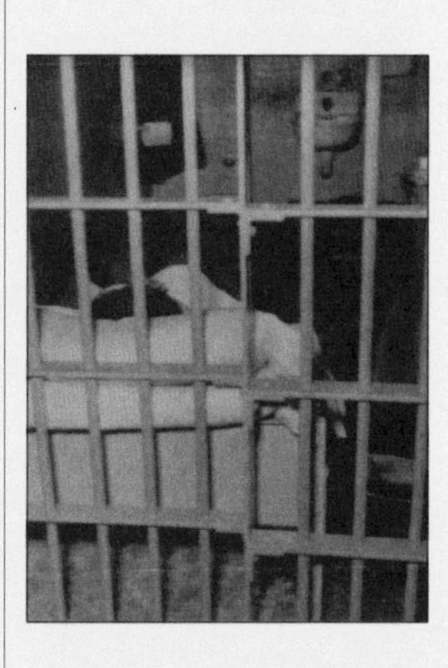

IN OTHER NEWS

✦ BOND, JAMES BOND. ✦
Dr. No, the first in what producers say will be a long list of James Bond films, continues to enthrall moviegoers. See MOVIES.

✦ SATELLITES IN SPACE? ✦
AT&T and Bell Telecommunications launch an experimental satellite called Telstar, which will orbit Earth. Satellite will enable television images and phone conversations to cross oceans. See TECHNOLOGY.

✦ ETCH-A-SKETCH ✦ MANIA
Kids are emptying toy store shelves of popular new "Etch-A-Sketch" toy, which enables users to erase their own drawings by shaking the toy up and down. See TOYS AND GAMES.

HAVE YOU SEEN THEM?

THE FBI RELEASED THE FOLLOWING DESCRIPTIONS OF THE ALCATRAZ ESCAPEES:

JOHN ANGLIN: age 32, height 5'10" (175 cm), weight 140 pounds (63 kg), blue eyes, blond hair, medium build, small scar on left check, round scar on left forearm.

CLARENCE ANGLIN: age 31, height 5'11" (177 cm), weight 168 pounds (76 kg), hazel eyes, light complexion, "ZONA" tattoo on left wrist, "NITA" tattoo on right forearm.

FRANK LEE MORRIS: age 35, height 5'7" (167 cm), weight 135 pounds (61 kg), hazel eyes, black hair. Tattoos include the number "13" at the base of the left index finger.

(continued from page 1)

when they went to wake them they found, under the covers of each cot, a fake head made from plaster with a painted face and hair presumably taken from the prison barber. Pillows had been laid under the covers to look like the convicts' sleeping bodies.

"The guards check the beds throughout the night, but they're looking for empty beds," Bars explained. "These beds looked like there were men sleeping in them."

It appears that sometime after 9:30 p.m. on Monday night, the convicts simultaneously squeezed through 18-inch (45 cm) holes hidden behind mesh-covered air vents in their cells. It then appears the men climbed through the vents and out onto the roof of the prison, where they slid down drainpipes to the ground. From there they somehow climbed over the two 12-foot (3.6 m) barbed-wire fences and ran toward the water.

"They were in clear view of the lookout tower the whole time," said prison worker Eugene Searchlight. "The guards must have been looking away at the exact moments they slid down and ran. They were either lightning-speed fast or they had impeccable timing."

How they got off the island—if they got off—is unknown. It is possible they are hiding inside one of the island's many caves. Perhaps, as some reports have suggested, they attempted to paddle to the nearby San Francisco shoreline using homemade rafts.

"The tides are pretty rough and the current makes for tough paddling," said San Francisco native Skipper Shore, who owns a sailboat in the local marina. "If I were to guess, I'd say they drowned in the bay."

If they did make it to shore, the men will be the first to ever successfully escape from Alcatraz Island. ■

ANATOMY OF ALCATRAZ

The Mysterious Times

September 25, 1964 | Volume CXVII No. 40 | Price: 20 cents

DID LEE HARVEY OSWALD KILL KENNEDY?

FEDERAL COMMISSION SAYS YES

Thousands of people lined the streets as Kennedy's motorcade made its way through downtown Dallas.

WASHINGTON, D.C. – Despite a growing web of conspiracy theories concerning last year's tragic assassination of President John F. Kennedy, a government commission has concluded that Lee Harvey Oswald, a book clerk at the Texas School Book Depository, acted alone when killing the president.

The conclusion was made in an 888-page report released yesterday by the Warren Commission, the agency assigned to investigate the facts surrounding the Kennedy assassination.

It was about 12:30 p.m. on November 22, 1963, when President Kennedy was shot while riding in his motorcade through a crowd of more than 200,000 people in downtown Dallas.

Authorities said the shots were fired from the sixth floor window of the Book Depository. Oswald, 24, was arrested at a nearby movie theater about an hour later. He was also accused of killing a police officer who had been shot shortly after the president's assassination. But the biggest problem in the case was that nobody saw him do it.

"We've got a few things that point to Oswald being our guy, but nothing definite," said a law enforcement agent who refused to give his name. "Is Oswald guilty beyond a shadow of a doubt? I don't know."

Police say they know this much for sure: A gunman fired three shots into the president's motorcade, killing Kennedy and injuring Texas Governor John B. Connally, who was sitting in the front seat of the open limousine.

Thousands of people saw it happen. Nobody saw the shooter.

Most witnesses reported hearing the shots coming from the direction of the Book Depository. Upon searching the building, police found on the sixth floor a rifle, a barricade of boxes, three used bullet cartridges, and a paper bag.

According to officials, Oswald's fingerprints were on the boxes, and a faint trace of his prints was found on the discarded rifle. In addition, witnesses said they saw Oswald on the sixth floor about 35 minutes before the shooting. He was also seen in the second-floor lunchroom a few minutes after the shooting.

(continued on page 2)

IN OTHER NEWS

✦ A G.I. NAMED JOE ✦

G.I. Joe, an action figure built to look like an American soldier, is now on every little boy's Christmas wish list. Find out where to buy the popular toy. See TRENDS.

✦ HUMAN RIGHTS ✦ LEADER SPEAKS OUT FROM HIS PRISON CELL

Read a letter from peace activist Nelson Mandela, who was sentenced to life in prison for fighting the apartheid movement in South Africa. See WORLD NEWS.

✦ BEATLEMANIA ✦

Read our interview with Paul McCartney, a member of the British band called The Beatles, who are quickly becoming rock 'n' roll's next big thing. See MUSIC.

Federal Commission declares Oswald guilty.

"But that's not unusual," said a Dallas resident. "He worked there. Of course he's going to be seen in the building."

"Maybe Oswald did it," said Grimace Horton, a Dallas history professor, "but I think there was someone helping him."

So do lots of others. A growing theory is that the assassination was a CIA-backed attempt to remove the controversial president from office. Other possible theories being proposed include Oswald acting as an agent of Fidel Castro, the KGB orchestrating the assassination in retaliation for the Cuban missile crisis, and even a U.S.-based shadow government opposed to President Kennedy's policies. Some witnesses believe there was a second gunman, saying they heard another shot fired from the top of a grassy knoll in front of and to the right of the presidential limousine. Nobody saw this alleged second gunman, however, and the Warren Commission says there is no evidence that he exists.

Oswald never admitted to the crime. He was shot by local nightclub owner Jack Ruby on November 24 during a prison transfer. Ruby said he killed Oswald out of anger and grief over the president's death. He is currently in prison awaiting trial.

"Until we find evidence to say otherwise, I think it's safe to say that Lee Harvey Oswald killed President Kennedy," said a Dallas local law enforcement agent.

The president, who was 46 when he was killed, is survived by his wife, Jacqueline, a 3-year-old son, John Jr., and a 6-year-old daughter, Caroline. ■

Many witnesses claim they heard shots coming from a "grassy knoll" (1) in front of the motorcade. Oswald allegedly fired fatal shots from a window of the Texas Book Depository (2). President's limousine was at (3) when first shot was fired. If "grassy knoll" theory holds, there must have been more than one assassin.

BE YOUR OWN DETECTIVE

Oswald's fingerprints are among the most important pieces of evidence against him. Everybody's fingerprints are different. Try dusting your own at home! (Be sure to ask for permission first.)

WARNING:
Some powders and makeup may stain fabrics.

What you'll need:

- Newspaper to protect the surface from mess
- A makeup brush
- Dark eye shadow (in powder form)
- A glass plate
- Transparent tape

What to do:

1. Lay down several sheets of paper to protect your work area.
2. Press your finger against the glass plate to leave your fingerprint (don't wash your hands first; the oilier the better!).
3. Dip the makeup brush in the eye-shadow powder.
4. Dust the powder lightly over the print.
5. Lightly blow off the excess powder. A darkened print should be left behind.
6. Take a strip of tape and press it carefully against the print.
7. Remove the tape slowly and you'll see that the print has been transferred to the tape.

Plain Arch

Plain Whorl

Central Pocket Loop

Loop

Accidental

Double Loop

Some fingerprint patterns as classified by the Federal Bureau of Investigation, United States Department of Justice

MR. DICTIONARY SAYS . . .

Conspiracy: **(1)** An agreement to perform together an illegal or wrongful act; **(2)** a joining or acting together, as if by sinister design.

The Mysterious Times

December 30, 1966 | Volume CXX No. 52 | Price: 25 cents

TEENAGE SWINDLER STILL ON THE RUN!

HOW DOES HE DO IT?

Posing as a Pan Am pilot was just one of Abagnale's disguises.

WASHINGTON, D.C. – The con artist who has successfully eluded police for almost three years, stealing an estimated $2.5 million dollars by posing as an airline pilot and cashing phony checks, is only a teenager, authorities have learned.

Investigators believe the swindler, whose name is Frank W. Abagnale, Jr., is about 18 or 19 years old. It is thought he began his moneymaking scheme when he was just 16.

"We don't know how he does it," said a law enforcement official close to the investigation. "When I was his age, I was playing baseball in my backyard and planning for college.

(continued on page 2)

IN OTHER NEWS

✦ CASUALTIES RISE ✦ IN VIETNAM

Reports show that as many as 5,008 U.S. troops have been killed in Vietnam since the beginning of the year. See WORLD NEWS.

✦ RACE FOR THE MOON! ✦

NASA says it will be ready to send country's first man to the moon by the end of the decade. Astronaut Neil Armstrong eyed for the job. See TECHNOLOGY.

✦ MINI'S STILL MAJOR ✦

The "Mini Skirt" is more popular than ever. These supershort skirts reveal a whole lot of leg, and everyone's wearing them. See FASHION.

HAVE YOU SEEN THIS MAN?

ABAGNALE is going by the name FRANK WILLIAMS. He has been known to pose as an airline pilot, a doctor, and a legal assistant. Anyone with information is urged to call his or her local police station.

(continued from page 1)
This kid is making a fortune as a con man and he doesn't even have a high school diploma."

According to recent reports, Abagnale began his criminal career cashing bad checks at banks in New York City, where he lived for a short while. He initially overdrew from his own bank account by thousands of dollars.

Before bank officials could catch up with him, he moved out of New York and changed his name to Frank Williams.

"Using his own checkbook, it was too easy to get caught," said a law enforcement official. "He needed to find a new way to make money."

In a stroke of what many onlookers have called pure genius, Abagnale decided to pose as a Pan American airline pilot. He bought a uniform, learned a little about the aviation industry, and began manufacturing his own Pan Am checks that he would cash mostly at hotels.

"It was a perfect plan," said Professor I.V. Lied, a New York criminologist. "Everybody loves airline pilots; they're like movie stars. When he walks in wearing a Pan Am uniform, who's going to question him?"

Nobody, apparently. Frank's plan has worked smoothly so far. During the past two years, the teenager has traveled the country cashing phony Pan Am paychecks and earning hundreds of thousands of dollars. But the F.B.I. has been on his trail almost since the beginning.

About two years ago in Miami, Abagnale was taken in for questioning by Dade County police officers. Throughout the interview he maintained he was Frank Williams, the pilot.

He allegedly produced fake identification and gave police several airline industry contacts to call. Apparently Frank had lied so convincingly that he had gained friends in the business. After finding nothing suspicious, officers reportedly apologized for taking up his time and let Abagnale go.

It was a close call for Frank, and one that law enforcement officials say won't happen again. According to a *Mysterious Times* source, agents are closing in on the con man, and expect he'll be in federal custody in the next few months.

Abagnale has also posed as a doctor, working for a brief period in an Atlanta hospital. In addition, he passed the bar exam in Louisiana and worked there as a legal assistant.

If caught, Abagnale faces at least 12 years in prison. ■

MR. DICTIONARY SAYS . . .

Con artist (also con man):
A swindler who exploits the confidence of his victim.

HOW TO SPOT A LIAR:

BY DR. JEN U. ENN, STAFF LIE DETECTOR

Frank Abagnale, Jr., has been able to mislead hundreds of people posing as an airline pilot, doctor, and legal assistant. Could you be fooled, too? Not if you know these easy tricks for spotting a liar by his or her body language.

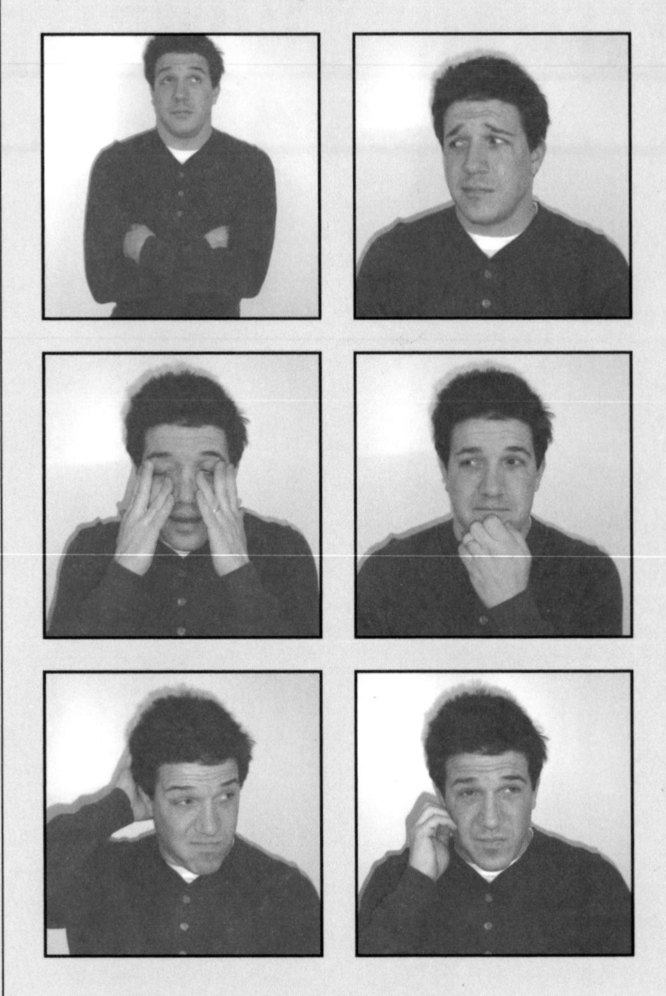

Someone who is lying may exhibit one or more of the following behaviors:

- rapid eye movement
- crossed arms
- fidgeting
- tendency to gaze to the right side (the creative side of the brain)
- rubbing eyes
- touching face
- playing with hair
- tugging at ear

The Mysterious Times

November 1, 1967 | Volume CXXI No. 44 | Price: 25 cents

FILMMAKER CAPTURES PHOTOS OF "BIGFOOT"

APELIKE BEAST CONTINUES TREK ACROSS CALIFORNIA WOODLANDS

A large ape-like creature is shown in Patterson's controversial film.

BLUFF CREEK, CALIFORNIA Bigfoot. Sasquatch. Call it what you will, but some Northern California residents say it's real, and that they've got the footage to prove it.

Last month, in the thickly wooded forest about 300 miles (480 km) north of San Francisco, veteran Sasquatch hunter Roger Patterson says he spotted the legendary man-ape stomping through a clearing. With 16-millimeter movie camera in hand, Patterson captured the creature as it loped back into the woods.

The grainy footage shows what looks like an eight-foot (2.4 m) tall gorilla swinging its long, furry arms and striding through the clearing with an upright gait as it quickly retreats into the cloak of the forest. Most primates, excluding humans, use their arms to walk, but the Sasquatch is said to be bipedal, meaning it walks on two legs. "This is not a hoax," says Bigfoot believer Timothy Wrangler, who has seen the footage. "If this was just a man in an ape suit, you wouldn't get the subtle curves of the muscles. You wouldn't get the perfect gorillalike posture. I think this is the real thing."

Sasquatch supporters contend the jerky, one-minute film is the most persuasive piece of evidence to support the mythical creature's existence ever found.

In Patterson's film, the so-called Sasquatch is close enough to show its muscles

(continued on page 2)

IN OTHER NEWS

✦ WAR'S DEATH ✦ TOLL RISES

U.S. military reports show more than 17,000 soldiers have died in Vietnam since 1961. As the war rages on, thousands continue to protest throughout the country. See POLITICS.

✦ BEAR NECESSITIES ✦

Disney's *The Jungle Book* continues to rake in dollars at the box office. The animated film, released last month, is still the top movie in the country. See ENTERTAINMENT.

✦ HAVE A HEART ✦

South African doctor Christiaan Barnard is optimistic about the first human heart transplant, set to be performed in Groote Schuur Hospital in Cape Town. The patient, a 55-year-old diabetic with incurable heart disease, was given the choice between certain death and the risky transplant surgery. He chose the surgery, which carries a 20 percent survival rate. See HEALTH.

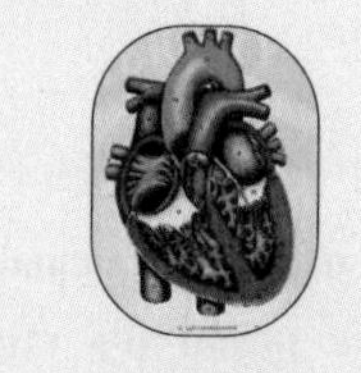

Left: *Alleged Bigfoot footprint reveals larger than man-sized feet.*

Below: *The huge footprints baffle the residents of Bluff Creek, California.*

(continued from page 1)

curve and ripple in the sunlight, but distant enough to leave the smaller details, specifically the facial features, open for interpretation.

The tape is real. But is it really Bigfoot?

"Show me the body of a Sasquatch and I'll believe it's real," said Dr. Julianne Ramirez, who specializes in the study of large primates. "This tape could just as easily be a man in an ape suit. It proves nothing."

Many other scientists share Ramirez's doubt, saying the tape's just too fuzzy to prove anything.

Indeed, the footage still leaves much to the imagination, and despite the gritty subject matter, no live Bigfoot has ever been caught, nor have any remains ever been found. Before Patterson's tape, the only real "evidence" of Bigfoot has been a scattering of footprints found on the forest floor throughout the country.

For generations, people have claimed to see hairy giants galumphing through the woods in British Columbia, Ohio, Arkansas, and Florida. Settlers in Northern California talked of a race of large apes as far back as the 1880s. In 1890, Teddy Roosevelt referenced Bigfoot in his book, The Wilderness Hunter, writing of a trapper thought to have been killed by a mysterious man-beast.

"This animal is obviously a shy creature," says Stacey LaBelle, a University of Northern California graduate student who is focusing her studies on the history of Sasquatch. "Obviously, it's very good at keeping low profile. That's why we've never seen it. It's simply hiding from us." ■

ABOMINABLE SNOWMAN:

BIGFOOT'S DISTANT COUSIN

Sasquatch isn't the only super-sized ape allegedly strutting its way into local and scientific lore. In the Himalayas, villagers have believed in the Yeti, or the Abominable Snowman, for generations.

In 1889, 13-inch (32.5 cm) footprints in the snow fueled the Yeti legend, and subsequent sightings followed, including one alleged incident in which a man claimed to be rescued from the snow by the elusive animal.

The Yeti is described as being about eight feet (2.4 m) tall with dark hair and a particularly bad odor. It is also believed to be able to make itself invisible at will. No photos or videos have been taken of the creature, leaving most scientists to consider it a mere myth.

WHOSE FEET ARE THOSE?

Footprints have long fueled the legend of Bigfoot, but sometimes what look like those of a Sasquatch may be the prints of some other animal. Can you name the creature that made these footprints?

Moose • Elk • Deer • Bighorn Sheep • Horse • Bigfoot
Large Dog or Wolf • Coyote • Badger • Beaver

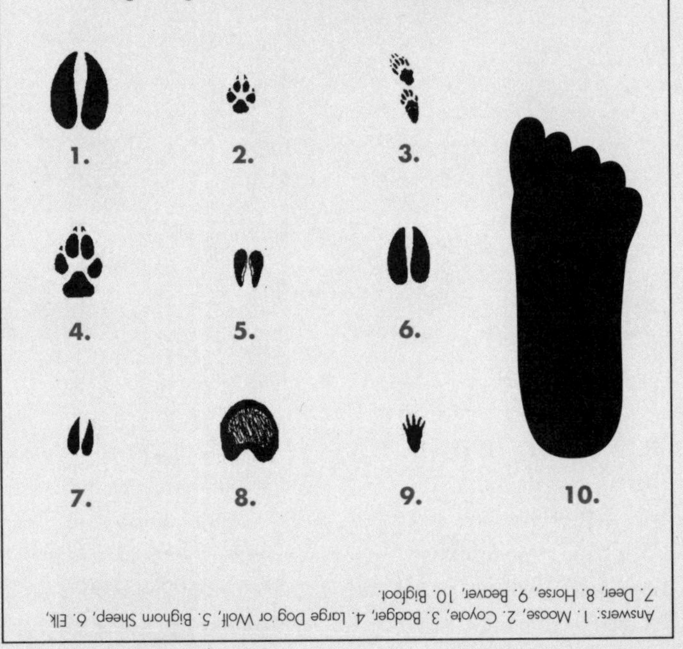

Answers: 1. Moose, 2. Coyote, 3. Badger, 4. Large Dog or Wolf, 5. Bighorn Sheep, 6. Elk, 7. Deer, 8. Horse, 9. Beaver, 10. Bigfoot.

The Mysterious Times

January 1, 1968 | Volume CXXII No. 1 | Price: 25 cents

POINT PLEASANT RESIDENTS STILL BELIEVE IN MYSTERIOUS "MOTHMAN"

Birdlike creature hasn't been seen since tragic bridge collapse; residents still ask: "What was it?"

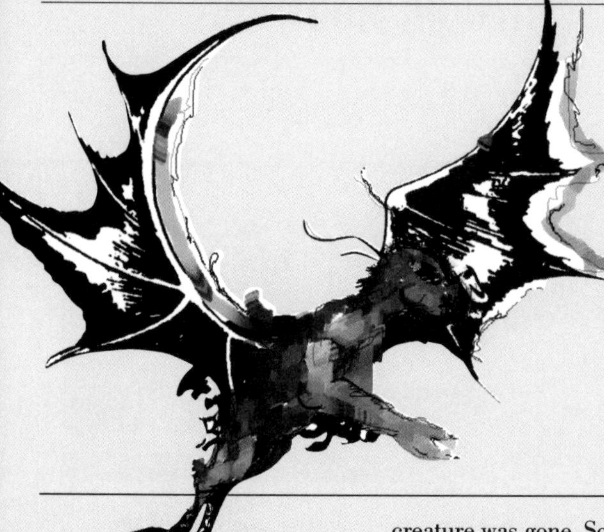

Left: *Artist's depiction of the Mothman based on a description by journalist John A. Keel.*
Above: *The Silver Bridge collapsed soon after the Mothman's appearances in Point Pleasant.*

POINT PLEASANT, WEST VIRGINIA – Almost a month after a bridge collapse that killed more than 40 people in the height of the holiday rush, many Mason County residents still cling to the idea that the tragedy was foreshadowed by a "birdlike" creature they call the "Mothman."

"People kept seeing this strange creature," said area resident Cindy Skare. "Then the bridge collapsed, and the creature was gone. Some people think maybe it was here to warn us about the danger."

The Mothman was first sighted on November 12, 1966. In the months to follow, area residents reported more than 100 additional sightings.

From start to finish, the events played like a Hollywood movie. According to reports, the first sighting happened in a cemetery near Clendenin, West Virginia, as five men were preparing a grave. The men claimed they saw a "brown human shape with wings" that allegedly flew over their heads.

But that was just the beginning. Three days later, four Point Pleasant residents reported seeing the Mothman while driving near a wildlife preserve outside of town. According to reports, the foursome saw a pair of glowing red eyes and a "thing" that was "shaped like a man, but bigger." All four witnesses described the creature as about seven feet (2.1 m) tall with wings folded against its back.

About a week later, four more people reportedly spotted the birdlike creature flying over their car and described its wingspan as about nine feet (2.7 m) wide. Its wings were described as "bat-like," and it supposedly emitted a humming sound as it flew. Residents speculate that the Mothman (so-named after a character in

(continued on page 2)

IN OTHER NEWS

✦ Texas Instruments ✦
Developing first handheld calculator; so-called "mini computer" to cost hundreds of dollars. See TECHNOLOGY.

✦ Vietnam War ✦
Protests continue across U.S.; casualty reports show that more than 17,000 soldiers have died since 1961. See WORLD NEWS.

✦ Film Review ✦
2001: A Space Odyssey— Movie depicts future filled with routine space travel, video phones, space stations, and moon landings. See ENTERTAINMENT.

(continued from page 1)

the Batman television series) may be hiding at an abandoned TNT plant, where explosives were stored during WWII. In November, a visitor to a home near the old plant was frightened by a "big gray thing" with "terrible glowing eyes." Another resident claimed she saw it in her backyard.

"These were respected members of the community saying they saw something that, as far as I know, doesn't exist," said local politician Gary Sputter. "I just can't see why they would be making it up."

But nobody can say for sure what the Mothman really is. Not a single photo has been taken as proof of its existence. Skeptics call the whole thing a case of mistaken identity.

"The residents of Point Pleasant probably saw something," said biologist Al J. Slimer. "But I don't think it was a huge flying monster."

Scientists speculate that given the town's proximity to the McClintic Wildlife Preserve, the Mothman is most likely a large bird. Wildlife experts have suggested it may be a sandhill crane. Snowy owls or Canada geese have also been suggested as possibilities.

Whether it's a bird or a monster with giant wings, the story has attracted national publicity, and journalists are descending on Point Pleasant.

"I want to believe in the Mothman," said photographer Seymour Snap. "But I need proof."

He may not have much luck. Sightings of the creature stopped a few weeks before the December 15 collapse of the Silver Bridge, which crosses the Ohio River from West Virginia into Ohio. Forty-six people died when the bridge buckled, plunging 31 cars into the icy water below.

The creature hasn't been seen in Point Pleasant since. In retrospect, some residents say the Mothman caused the tragedy; others attribute a more benevolent role to the odd creature.

"The Mothman never did hurt anyone," said Skare. "Maybe it was just here to warn us about the bridge."

"Point Pleasant is a small town," added Sputter. "To have these bizarre and tragic events happen around the same time—it just seems like there must be some connection." ■

Our Readers React

THE MYSTERIOUS TIMES ASKED OUR READERS:

Do you believe in the Mothman?

"What are you, some kind of nut?"

—*Curt Rudely, Age 32*
ATTORNEY

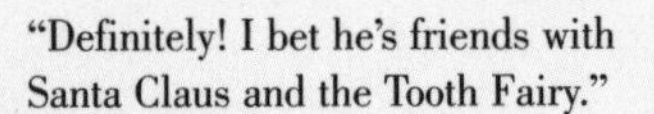

"Definitely! I bet he's friends with Santa Claus and the Tooth Fairy."

—*Buddy Jiles, Age 6*
FIRST GRADER

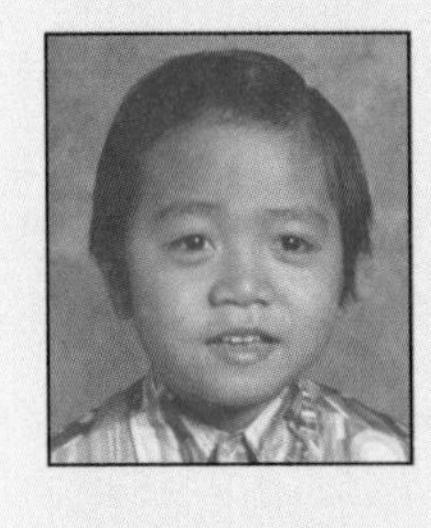

"Certainly not. It was obviously a stray specimen of *Nyctea scandizca*, or possibly, *Buteo lineatus*, but just as likely, *Grus canadensis* . . . wait a minute, where are you going? I'm not finished!"

—*Franken Feathers, Age 38*
BIRDWATCHER

Bird or Monster?

Here are a few birds wildlife experts say could be mistaken for the so-called "Mothman." What do you think?

BARN OWL
Color: Brown/white
Eyes: Brown
Height: 1–2 feet (30–60 cm)
Wingspan: 2–4 feet (60–120 cm)

CANADA GOOSE
Color: Brown/black/white
Eyes: Brown
Height: 2–3 feet (60–90 cm)
Wingspan: 3–4 feet (90–120 cm)

SANDHILL CRANE
Color: Gray with reddish patches around its eyes
Eyes: Yellow
Height: 4–5 feet (1.2–1.5 m)
Wingspan: 6–8 feet (1.8–2.4 m)

"MOTHMAN"
(as described by witnesses)
Color: Brownish-gray
Eyes: Red
Height: 7–8 feet (2.1–2.4 m)
Wingspan: 8–10 feet (2.4–3 m)

The Mysterious Times

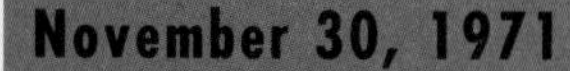

November 30, 1971 | **Volume CXXV No. 48** | **Price: 25 cents**

MAN JUMPS FROM PLANE WITH KNAPSACK OF CASH:

INVESTIGATORS SEARCH FOR SUSPECT

ARIEL, WASHINGTON – About 4 p.m. on Thanksgiving eve, a man boarded a plane bound for Seattle. He jumped out of it six hours later wearing a parachute and carrying $200,000 in stolen cash.

The high-flying thief, who identified himself to airline officials as Dan B. Cooper, has not yet been found, and law enforcement officials are calling the episode one of the most bizarre hijacking attempts on record.

It started at the Portland, Oregon, airport when a middle-aged, average-looking man wearing a dark suit, sunglasses, and a black necktie boarded Northwest Orient Airlines Flight 305 along with 35 other passengers.

Just before takeoff, Cooper passed stewardess Flo Schaffner a note. Miss Schaffner, thinking it was a request for her phone number, simply put it in her pocket. After takeoff, she opened the note to find it actually contained a bomb threat and a demand for $200,000 in a knapsack. He showed her what appeared to be sticks of

(continued on page 2)

Above: *A search party looks for the hijacker and the stolen money near the Washington/Oregon border.* Below: *The path of Flight 305 and the zone where the thief may have landed.*

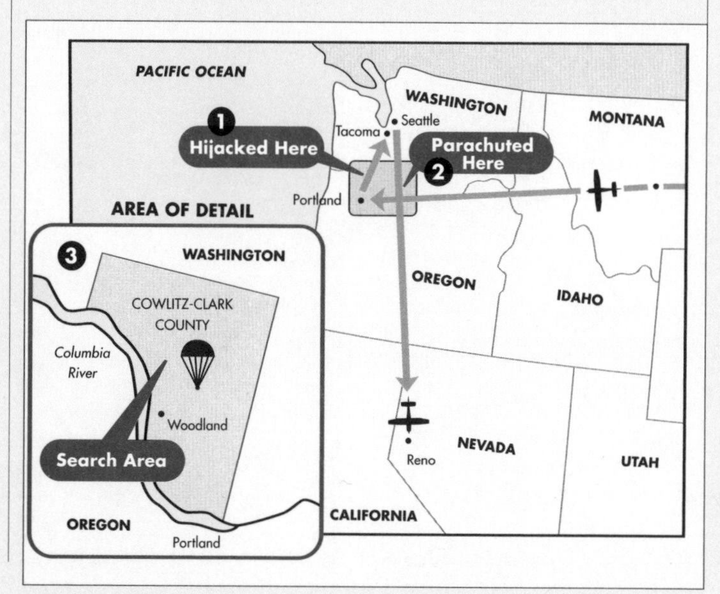

IN OTHER NEWS

✦ PONG WITHOUT ✦ THE PING?

Atari is developing a computer game called "Pong," modeled after the tabletop game Ping-Pong. It is scheduled for release next year. See TOYS AND GAMES.

✦ JACKSON FIVE ✦ STILL ON TOP

The Jackson Five is still topping the charts with their Motown single, "I Want You Back." Now that they have their own cartoon on ABC, the fivesome is winning even more hearts across the country. See MUSIC.

✦ FIGHTING ✦ FOR THE ENVIRONMENT

Project Greenpeace, an organization dedicated to helping the environment worldwide, is founded as a ship named the *Greenpeace* sets sail from Vancouver, British Columbia, intent on stopping a U.S. nuclear test in the Aleutian Islands. See ENVIRONMENT.

(continued from page 1)
dynamite in his briefcase and said he needed the items by 5 p.m. Cooper demanded that the plane land in Seattle, where he asked that four parachutes and the money be delivered in $20 bills, apparently having calculated that 10,000 $20 bills would weigh just 21 pounds (9.5 kg). He also requested the bills have random serial numbers so that they would be harder for the FBI to track.

Another clever detail: He ordered four parachutes. If he had ordered just one, the FBI might have given him a faulty chute in order to bring him down. With multiple chutes, officials worried Cooper might be taking a hostage. They couldn't risk it; all the parachutes had to be functional.

Once the plane landed in Seattle and the FBI had delivered all the requested items, Cooper let his fellow passengers and flight attendant Schaffner go, then ordered the pilot to take off for Mexico. He insisted that the plane fly no higher than 10,000 feet (3,000 m), which is about 20,000 feet (6,000 m) lower than it would normally fly. He also ordered the pilot to fly much more slowly than usual, and to keep the landing gear down. Around 7:45 p.m., Cooper asked the one remaining stewardess to show him how to open the back stairs of the 727. He then commanded her to go into the cockpit and stay there. At about 8 p.m., the pilot saw a red light on his instrument panel that indicated that a door was open; shortly afterwards, he felt a thump—Cooper had jumped from the plane into the dark, rainy night, presumably with the money strapped to his body.

Hundreds of FBI agents along with Army troops immediately rushed to the thickly wooded area near Ariel, Washington, over which Cooper had jumped. They found nothing—there was simply no trace of D. B. Cooper or the money.

The FBI does have one up on the skyjacker. In a few rushed hours they were able to microfilm every bill of Cooper's loot, so it can be traceable if spent. So far none of the bills has turned up.

Professional skydivers told *The Mysterious Times* that Cooper's jump was difficult but not impossible, especially if he had some previous experience jumping out of planes.

Meanwhile, the well-dressed, soft-spoken Cooper has become an instant legend.

The flight attendants all described Cooper's demeanor as that of a gentleman, portraying him as calm and polite.

"He didn't hurt anyone," said 13-year-old passenger Kay Swoon. "He's like a gentleman bandit, like Robin Hood. I think he's kind of cool."

HAVE YOU SEEN HIM?

The skyjacker of Flight 305 is described as around 45 years old and about six feet (2 m) tall, with an average build and dark hair. He identified himself as Dan Cooper, but FBI officials don't think that is his real name. Anyone with information is urged to call local authorities.

"We don't care if he was polite, or if he was wearing a top hat and tails," said police officer Burley Stone. "He is a criminal, and if we find him, he'll be jailed and prosecuted."

Anyone who has seen Cooper is asked to notify the FBI. A reward is being offered for any information leading to an arrest. ■

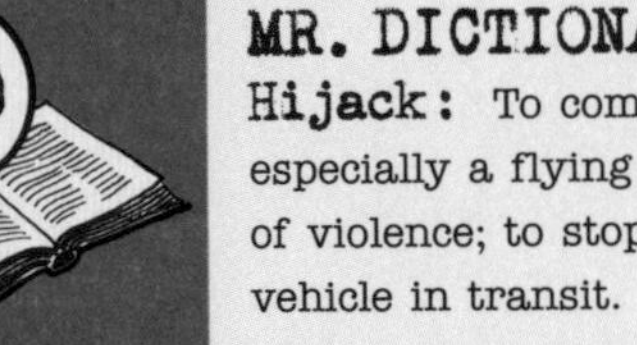

MR. DICTIONARY SAYS . . .

Hijack: To commandeer a vehicle, especially a flying airplane, by threat of violence; to stop and steal from a vehicle in transit.

THE MYSTERIOUS TIMES ASKED OUR READERS:

Is D. B. Cooper "Cool" or "Criminal"?

THE MYSTERIOUS TIMES

February 25, 1980 Volume CXXXIV No. 9 Price: 50 cents

SCIENTISTS CONTINUE SEARCH FOR LIVE GIANT SQUID "IT'S OUT THERE," THEY SAY

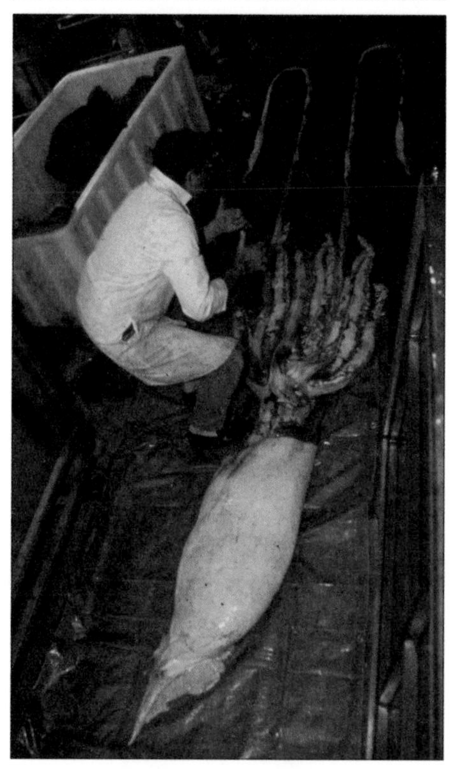

Giant squids have been found washed up on shores but never seen alive.

PLUM ISLAND, MASSACHUSSETTS Up to 60 feet (18 m) in length, with tentacles and a huge, beaklike mouth, it lives deep in the ocean, where it preys on whales—but no one has ever seen one alive. Is it a mythical sea monster, a creature from a fisherman's worst nightmare—or is it just another member of the squid family, albeit a big one?

The answer is hard to find, but science has just taken a step forward in the quest to discover the truth about *Architeuthis*, or the Giant Squid.

Last week, the body of one of the huge creatures washed up on the shores of Plum Island, making it one of no more than 50 *Architeuthis* carcasses to be found since the 1600s. Scientists have yet to see the gargantuan invertebrate alive and in its natural habitat, which is believed to be more than 6,600 feet (2,000 m) below the surface of the ocean.

"It was thrilling to find that squid," said marine biologist Delphine Flipper of Boston. "But really, we'd much rather see it in the water, alive."

It would seem unlikely that a creature that can weigh up to 2,000 pounds (900 kg) would be hard to find.

"We know they're out there," said Flipper, adding that the squid found last week was a smaller specimen, at about 30 feet (9 m). "We just need to look a little harder and go a little deeper."

Deeper, that is, into the water. Even the best deep-sea divers can only swim to about 500 feet (150 m), while submarines can reach about 3,000 feet (900 m) below the surface. That is still far above the Giant Squid's home depth.

Until the late 1800s, the Giant Squid was considered to be a myth, a product of the fevered minds of those out at sea for long periods of time. Although numerous fishermen over the years claimed to have encountered a gigantic, tentacled creature far out to sea, no one could substantiate their tales. French author Jules Verne was inspired by the accounts to write the story of Captain Nemo and his meeting with a squid "of colossal dimensions" in *20,000 Leagues Under the Sea*. Carcasses had washed ashore from time to time, but not until 1874 was a Giant Squid first inspected by scientists, after a Rev. Moses Harvey of Newfoundland bought a corpse of one from some fishermen, and Yale University Professor A. E. Verrill examined it in his lab.

Today, ironically, scientists say they know more about dinosaurs than they do about the Giant Squid. Without the opportunity to observe a live

(continued on page 2)

IN OTHER NEWS

✦ OIL SPILL ✦
An oil tanker explosion off Pilos, Greece, causes a huge oil spill. Environmentalists fear for lives of local sea animals. See SCIENCE.

✦ I WANT MY MTV! ✦
"Music Television," a.k.a. "MTV," is gearing up to hit the cable airwaves. The channel, to debut in August, will present "music videos" of popular and up-and-coming bands. See TELEVISION.

✦ THE TORCH IS OUT ✦
The Winter Olympics wrap up in Lake Placid, New York. The event featured 1,072 athletes from 37 countries. The next winter Olympics will be held in Yugoslavia in 1984. See SPORTS.

(continued from page 1)
squid, and understand its behavior, including how it mates and how it interacts with other marine life, everything is still open for interpretation.

"Dissecting the dead squids can only tell us so much," says marine biologist Kallie Mari.

But scientists aren't completely in the dark. For one thing, the Giant Squid, which is the world's largest invertebrate, has the most complex brain of any invertebrate. Along with its volleyball-sized eyes, the animal has eight arms, each the width of a large snake, covered with 200 to 300 suckers that act like suction cups to help the squid grip its food. It also has two feeding tentacles that extend far from its body that it uses to nab its prey.

The Giant Squid shares the cephalopod class of invertebrates with other marine life including the cuttlefish, the octopus, and, of course, those yummy little squids you're likely to see fried up and served as "calamari" at your favorite restaurant.

Until science goes deep into the ocean, the rest will remain a mystery. ■

YUM . . . SQUID

Squid isn't just for deep-water studies. Another kind of squid (while not the "giant" kind) is actually pretty tasty. Next time you're at a restaurant try ordering the following dishes (note: squid and calamari are the same thing):

- squid salad
- fried squid (ALSO KNOWN AS FRIED CALAMARI);
- baked squid
- barbecued squid
- calamari sticks

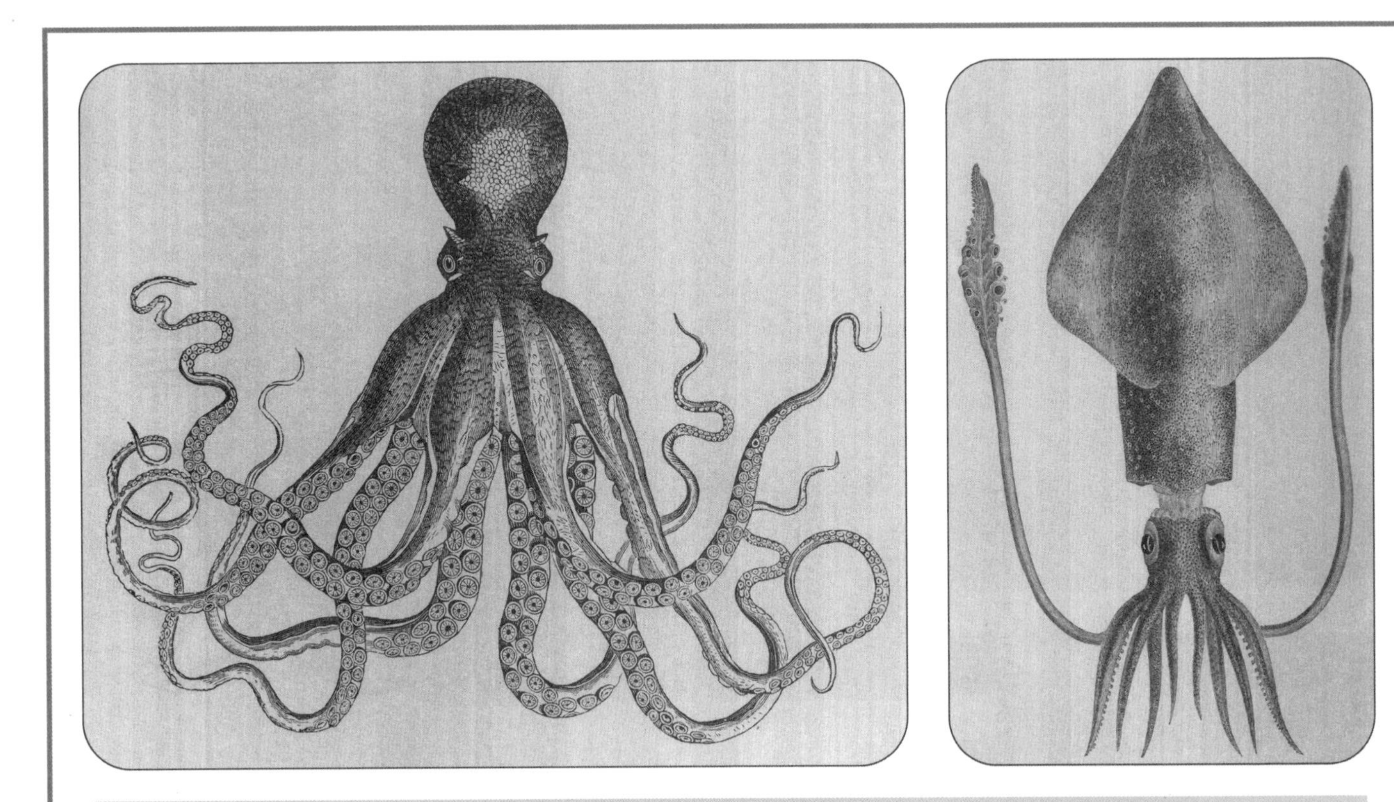

SQUID VS. OCTOPUS: WHAT'S THE DIFFERENCE?

Squids and octopuses (or "octopi") are both in the class named Cephalopoda, meaning "head-footed" (they both move head-first). The two creatures have many similarities, but their main difference lies in their numbers of "arms": an octopus has eight of them while a squid has ten. The squid's extra two arms, called tentacles, stretch longer than the rest and are used to grab prey. On both the octopus and the squid the arms are covered with hundreds of tiny suckers used to latch onto food.

September 20, 1991 Volume XLV No. 37 Price: 75 cents

CROP CIRCLE CREATORS COME FORWARD

OTHER FIELD FORMATIONS STILL A MYSTERY

WILTSHIRE, ENGLAND – For years people all over the world have believed that a rash of strange crop formations in southern England's rural countryside were the work of some unknown, extraterrestrial force. Now it appears the alleged alien artwork was just a hoax.

Doug Bower and Dave Chorley, a pair of elderly British UFO enthusiasts and artists, admitted earlier this month that they had created many of the first "crop circles" seen in the U.K. The pair said they used planks of wood connected to ropes, called "stalk-stompers," to make the patterns in the oat fields. They said they did it as a joke.

"I wish I had thought of that," said 17-year-old Bastian Mender, the son of a Wiltshire farmer. "Those two guys are famous now. Those crop circles had everyone screaming 'aliens.' I think it's hilarious."

It was Chorley and Bower's designs that threw the mystery of crop circles into the spotlight in the late 1970s. Their patterns consisted of simple circles in oat fields formed by acres of flattened plants amid uniform stretches of farmland. The patterns often appeared overnight, covering large swathes of otherwise untouched fields. Many people suspected they were created by extraterrestrials, beliving the designs to be forms of alien communication. They were also thought to be spacecraft landing pads or intraplanetary maps.

Above: *Some have speculated that crop circles are the work of aliens.*

"All this time people have thought it was the work of aliens," said British sociologist Miles Chartwell. "Really it was just the work of artists."

But the mystery is not completely explained. While Chorley and Bower may have made some of the crop circles, their oat-laden masterpieces are only part of the story. Since the 1970s hundreds of other crop formations have appeared all over the world, getting more and more complex as the years go by.

Smaller circles are a few yards wide but many enormous circles that can only be fully seen from the air have also been documented. This past summer, some 600 circles were counted, including a Celtic cross design in front of British Prime Minister John Major's home (probably a hoax) and a

(continued on page 2)

IN OTHER NEWS

✦ A WEB OF OUR OWN? ✦

Find out more about the "World Wide Web," a new kind of computer-based technology that will allow users to connect with people and information all over the world from the comfort of their home computers. See TECHNOLOGY.

✦ KIDS IN SOUTH ✦ AFRICA SPEAK OUT

Find out what it's like for kids growing up in South Africa now that the country has ended its 42-year system of racial segregation called apartheid. See WORLD VIEWS.

✦ FLANNEL ISN'T ✦ JUST FOR P.J.'S

"Grunge" fashion, marked by flannel shirts and big, clunky shoes, is becoming more and more popular. The fad started in Seattle and is quickly reaching the youth of America. See FASHION.

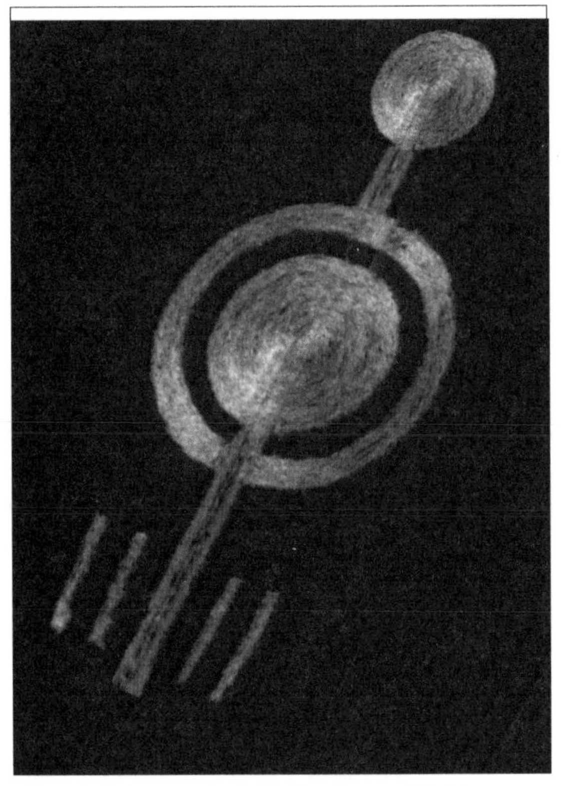

Above: *Crop circle in a canola field, West Kennet, Wiltshire.*

(continued from page 1)

12,000-square yard (9,600 sq. m) design that appeared near Barbury Castle, where local residents reported seeing mysterious lights, a loud rumbling, and power outages.

Most of the formations seen today—and there are hundreds every year—incorporate rings, symbols, straight and curved lines, and shapes so precise they appear to follow strict mathematical formulas.

Some say the exactitude of the patterns and the speed with which they're created makes them a nearly impossible feat for human hands. And, in some cases the plants inside the patterns are physically different than the plants outside the patterns, a detail that scientists have yet to explain.

And there are other strange incidents. People have said they witnessed mysterious lights, felt tingling sensations, and experienced shocks big enough to knock them over, all in the vicinity of crop circles.

Meanwhile, cereologists—those who study crop circles—don't dismiss the human element, saying at least 90 percent of crop circles are clearly man-made. It's the other 10 percent that leaves them wondering.

"How do you get into and out of a field without leaving any trace of footprints?" asked Willie Aud, a local cereologist. "Especially if you're carrying heavy equipment, the kind of equipment that may be needed to flatten 1,000 feet (300 m) of farmland."

With hoaxers confusing the issue, believers and skeptics are equally determined to hold their positions. This is a mystery no closer to being solved. ■

SEE THEM BY AIR!

Sure you've seen them in the papers, but nothing beats the experience of seeing England's famous crop circles by air-conditioned helicopter.

CROPAir, a new tourism company based in London, is now offering 45-minute rides over some of the country's most exquisite crop formations. As you hover over the decorated fields of corn and wheat, "Mr. Croppy," a London native and crop-circle expert, leads a narrated tour.

Tour packages start at just £8,900 and are available only to those who know the secret password. For more information, contact CROPAir at 555 Circle Drive, England.

MR. DICTIONARY SAYS...
Crop: A group of cultivated plants or agricultural produce, such as grain, vegetables, or fruit.

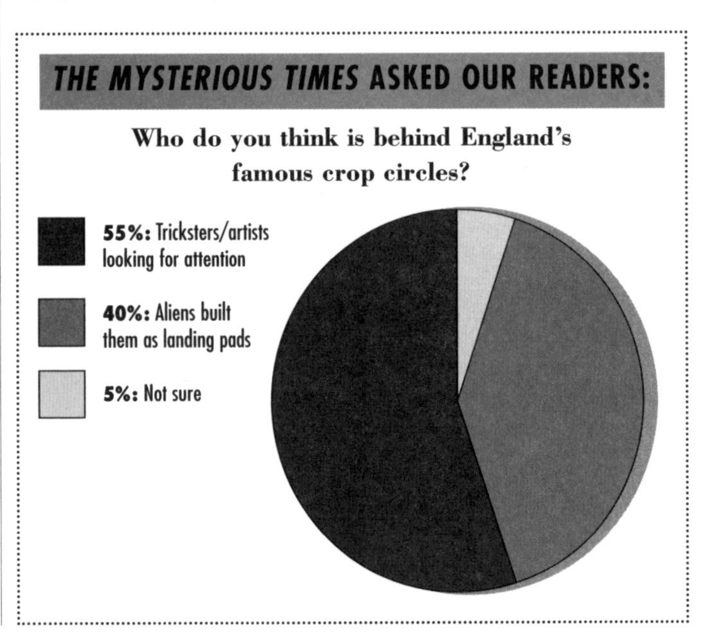

THE MYSTERIOUS TIMES

March 18, 1995 | Volume XLIX No. 11 | Price: 75 cents

PRECIOUS ARTWORKS STILL MISSING FIVE YEARS LATER

AUTHORITIES NO CLOSER TO CATCHING THIEVES

The Isabella Stewart Gardner Museum was robbed of more than $300 million dollars' worth of art.

BOSTON, MASSACHUSETTS – It has been five years to the day since two men snuck into Boston's Isabella Stewart Gardner Museum shortly after midnight and made off with more than $300 million in treasured artworks. Today, authorities are no closer to solving the crime, which has been called the greatest art heist of the 20th century.

The March 18, 1990, break-in left the museum, an aging facility designed to look like a Venetian palace, robbed of 13 prized pieces of art, including works by Vermeer, Manet, five by Degas, and three by Rembrandt. The stolen works included 11 sketches and paintings, a 3,000-year-old Chinese beaker, and the bronzed top of a Napoleonic flagstaff.

"How do two men break into an art museum and escape with $300 million in artwork without being caught?" wondered police officer Louis Brush.

The thieves' plan, as it turned out, was brilliantly simple. According to authorities, the thieves managed to sneak in-side the museum at 1:24 a.m. by posing as Boston police officers.

Wearing fake police uniforms probably rented from a costume store, the thieves told on-duty security guards that they were responding to a call of a disturbance in the area. Contrary to museum policy, the *(continued on page 2)*

HAVE YOU SEEN THESE PAINTINGS?

BY PROFESSOR ELLA EASEL, STAFF ART CRITIC

STORM ON THE SEA OF GALILEE
(OIL ON CANVAS, 1633)
Rembrandt's only sea-scape is an interpretation of the biblical story of Jesus and his disciples caught at sea in a powerful storm. As the boat pitches wildly, Jesus quells the waves and saves his disciples.

THE CONCERT
(OIL ON CANVAS, 1658–1660)
One of only 36 known paintings by the artist Johannes "Jan" Vermeer, the painting shows a man playing a lute, a young woman on a harpsichord, and another man singing.

CHEZ TORTONI
(OIL ON CANVAS, 1878–1880)
A self-portrait by the French Impressionist Edouard Manet depicting him sketching at a table in the Café Tortoni in Paris.

(continued from page 1)
guards let the thieves into the building.

In the guards' defense, a friend said, "The guards thought they were cops. They were just trying to keep the museum safe."

Once they were inside, the thieves tied up the guards and put them in the basement. According to the FBI, no weapons were used throughout the robbery. Two hours later, just the empty frames of the stolen masterpieces hung on gallery walls. The thieves had also managed to take the video surveillance tape before escaping with their prized loot.

Together the stolen art is worth as much as $300 million. Among the most precious of the missing works are Rembrandt's *Storm on the Sea of Galilee*, and a tiny etching, a rare and priceless self-portrait of the master. The least valuable work was a metal eagle that crowned the top of a Napoleonic battle flag; some experts believe the thieves took this object as a kind of "battle prize."

The FBI has considered various angles on the case, from organized crime to international smuggling rings, but nothing has brought police closer to catching the suspects or recovering the artwork.

"It's strange. You'd think one of the paintings would have turned up by now," said Priscilla Frame, who works at a New York City art gallery. "Nobody's reported a single sighting of any of them."

The Gardner museum has offered a reward of $1 million for any information leading to the recovery of the stolen artwork. So far almost 2,000 tips have come in from around the world, but none have panned out. "Somebody out there must have seen these works," said a museum spokesperson. "Somebody will eventually come forward."

But the outlook isn't good. According to statistics, about 90 percent of stolen art is never found. "We're not overly optimistic," admitted a Boston police officer. "But we won't give up looking."

The FBI has more information about the heist, including detailed descriptions of the suspects and photos of the artwork, on its website at http://www.fbi.gov. ■

DO YOU KNOW YOUR ARTWORK?

In 1911 Leonardo da Vinci's *Mona Lisa* was stolen from the Louvre Museum in Paris. Authorities recovered the priceless masterpiece 27 months later when the thief tried to sell it to an Italian museum.

Would you recognize the famed painting if you saw it?
Test your art knowledge. Which of the paintings below is the real *Mona Lisa?*

Answer: The real *Mona Lisa* is in the middle.

OTHER ART HEISTS

December 1988: Three Van Gogh paintings, worth up to $90 million, were stolen from the Kroller-Muller Museum in Holland by thieves who entered via an unlocked window. They returned one; police retrieved the others.

May 1988: A Van Gogh, a Cézanne, and a Johan Jongkind painting, together worth about $52 million, were stolen from the Stedelijk Museum in Amsterdam. Police found the art 11 days later.

May 1986: Eighteen works, by Vermeer, Gainsborough, Goya, and Rubens, were stolen from a home in Ireland by Dublin-based gangster Martin Cahill. The art is worth $40 million. One of the stolen paintings was found; ten are still missing.

October 1985: Nine paintings, including a Monet, a Renoir, and a Morisot, together worth $80 million, were stolen from the Marmottan Museum in Paris. None were recovered.

June 20, 1997 Volume LI No. 24 Price: 75 cents

HOLD ON TO YOUR UMBRELLAS, IT'S RAINING TOADS!

Above: *Toads and frogs are light enough to be picked up by strong winds and dropped from the sky like rain.*
Left: *Here it is "raining" rats!*

VILLA ANGEL FLORES, MEXICO – Ever heard the expression, "raining cats and dogs?" It rained toads in this small northern Mexican town Saturday night. That's right: Toads.

The amphibious downpour apparently began in the late evening, with motorists reporting toads dropping from the sky at around 11 p.m. The falling creatures were pelting windshields and splatting on sidewalks throughout the town.

"I thought someone was throwing rocks at my car," said Miguel LaRana, who was driving to his job at a local health clinic when the toads began falling. "But then I realized they were toads. Dead toads! It was horrifying."

Some would say the storm was the sign of something ominous. Others would say it's just the weather.

"Admittedly it is one of the odder events of nature," said San Francisco meteorologist Scott Rainy. "It doesn't happen often, but it happens."

Meteorologists say it's not unheard of for animals, insects, or other out-of-place objects to rain from the sky. But unlike true rain, which is created inside the clouds, animal downpours originate elsewhere. High winds are to blame for this phenomenon, according to Rainy. "The toads are being lifted off the ground and dumped down somewhere they don't belong. The wind acts like a net—it just scoops them up."

What happens, scientists say, is that tornadoes or other powerful wind gusts lift the creatures from their native habitats, generally lakes, rivers and streams. When the storm loses its strength, all the debris that has been scooped up then plummets from the sky.

So, in the case of the Mexican toads, weather experts say a tornado must have sucked up the critters from a nearby pond or stream and dropped them

(continued on page 2)

IN OTHER NEWS

✦ BIG CHANGES COMING ✦ FOR HONG KONG

The countdown has begun in Hong Kong, where in ten days the country will become part of China. It has been under British control for 99 years. See WORLD NEWS.

✦ WOMEN ✦ IN BASKETBALL

The WNBA (Women's National Basketball Association) is set to start its season this fall. Read our interviews with some of the players. See SPORTS.

✦ YOU GO, GIRL! ✦

The Spice Girls, a British, five-piece girl band, hits the top of the charts. The spunky group, most popular with teenagers, is on track to become one of the highest-selling girl bands of all time. See MUSIC.

(continued from page 1)
down onto unsuspecting villagers miles away. Most of the toads were dead long before hitting the ground.

"It's a rare occurrence," Rainy said. "But people have described similar phenomena for thousands of years."

Dead birds, partially frozen, have reportedly been seen falling from the sky during hailstorms. Other non-water rains have included turtles, crabs, grasshoppers, and even alligators.

On July 4, 1995, residents of Keokuk, Iowa, looked outside to see soda cans pelting down. A tornado that hit a soft drink bottling plant 150 miles (240 km) away was responsible.

In biblical times, great "rains of blood" terrified many who believed in bad omens or punishments. But meteorologists say the red, seemingly "bloody," rains were nothing more menacing than sandstorms.

One such sandstorm occurred as recently as 1968, when a shower in southern England reportedly covered everything in red dust. Scientists say the dust came from the Sahara desert—nearly 1,000 miles (1,600 km) away—and was carried by clouds before falling in a reddish-colored rain shower.

"It's nothing to worry about," said meteorologist Dustin Sands. "Mother Nature has some pretty odd tricks up her sleeve, but I can assure you, there's nothing scary or ominous about them." ■

BE PREPARED!

Are you prepared should another toad-dropping disaster strike? Do you have an umbrella strong enough to protect you from storms of frogs or toads?

If your answer is No then you need a FROGBRELLA! Invented by Oddball Inc., the company that brought you BUGOFF Spray (a nontoxic spray used to repel pesky friends and relatives), FROGBRELLA provides an indispensable layer of protection against Mother Nature's less traditional weather phenomena, including rains of toads, frogs, dogs, cats, and small meteorites.

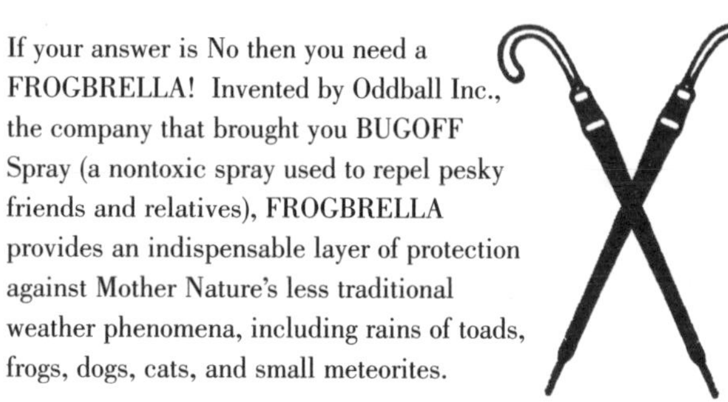

FROGBRELLA is made of pure stainless steel and weighs only 87 pounds (39 kg). It comes with a handy carrying case, made of iron.

The first 100 callers can receive the FROGBRELLA for just $200. act now! Call 555-FROG.

FROM TADPOLE TO TOAD

BY PROFESSOR PADMA, GUEST BIOLOGIST

◆ ◆ ◆

Believe it or not, toads (and frogs) aren't born looking like the croaking, jumpy little critters they are. Toads begin as tadpoles, tiny fishlike creatures that wiggle out of their eggs and live in ponds for their first few weeks of life. Initially they have gills and a tail, like a fish.

At about five weeks they sprout back legs and their gills start to disappear. At this point the tadpoles can still breathe underwater through gills inside their bodies. About a week after that, the tadpole develops lungs, which means it has to breathe air. Now, it must swim to the surface, but since it doesn't have front legs, it still lives in the water.

Soon its front legs start to appear, and its tail begins to absorb into its body. At about 14 weeks, the tadpole becomes a frog or toad and crawls out of the water to begin its life on land.

The Mysterious Times

December 4, 1999 | Volume LIII No. 21 | Price: 75 cents

UGANDAN BOY RAISED BY MONKEYS NOT SO DIFFERENT AFTER ALL

GOES FROM JUNGLE BOY TO SINGING SENSATION

KAMPALA, UGANDA – John Ssabunnya's life isn't unlike those of many 14-year-old boys. He plays video games. He sings in the school choir. He likes sports. The only difference (and it's a pretty big one): John was raised for three years by monkeys in the densely forested jungle of Uganda.

But before you picture the vine-swinging legend of Tarzan or Mowgli from *The Jungle Book*, understand this: John does not talk with the animals, and he doesn't dance through the forest dodging evil snakes and singing "The Bear Necessities."

"It's actually quite a sad story," said anthropologist Harry Ayp, who studies primates at a Los Angeles animal center. "People are fascinated by the idea, but they forget it's about a small child who basically lost his entire family. Twice."

According to reports, John's fate was born of tragedy. Born in the mid-1980s, he was abandoned in the dense jungle as a 2-year-old after his mother was murdered. Were it not for a colony of monkeys that was said to have stumbled upon the solitary child and taken him in, John probably would have died in the wild. It appears the group of African vervet monkeys adopted him as a member of their family.

Above: *Vervets are forest-dwellers, keeping to the safety of trees.*
Below: *Vervet fur ranges from silvery-gray to olive green.*

Vervet monkeys (also known as African green monkeys) are a class of medium-sized primates, weighing up to 17 pounds (27 kg). They are fairly intelligent and form "tribes" of 10 to 50 individuals. John apparently lived as they did, climbing trees and eating a diet of mostly nuts, fruits, and

(continued on page 2)

IN OTHER NEWS

✦ D'OH! ✦

The popular FOX television show *The Simpsons* recently celebrated its 10th anniversary. Read our interview with Bart and Marge Simpson. See TELEVISION.

✦ CROSSING THE OCEAN ✦ ONE STROKE AT A TIME

Eighty-one days and 2,962 miles (4,739 km) later, Tori Murden is now the first woman to have crossed the Atlantic Ocean by rowboat alone. Murden arrived in Guadeloupe yesterday; she started from the Canary Islands. See WORLD NEWS.

✦ COUNTDOWN ✦ TO THE MILLENNIUM

Computer analysts say the world need not worry about the clock striking midnight on December 31, 1999. Despite concerns that the changing century will mess up computer programs worldwide, experts say the fear is unjustified. See TECHNOLOGY.

(continued from page 1)
insects. It is believed he lived with the troop for about three years, until he was spotted by a local woman in 1991. When some villagers tried to retrieve the boy, not only did he resist capture but his adoptive family defended him, throwing sticks at the men as they grabbed the boy from the tree and took him back to their village.

"It was natural for them to protect him," Ayp said. "They thought humans were the enemies. They didn't want their 'child' to be taken away."

Flea-ridden, with long nails and hair, he was brought to the village and cleaned up. The boy was bruised and his knees were scarred, apparently from crawling; he was about five years old but could not yet walk. He also could not talk or cry. Someone recognized him as John Ssabunnya, whose parents were both dead.

He was taken to an orphanage, where he learned to speak and how to live with other human beings. Once he began talking, it was discovered that the former wild child had a lovely singing voice. Now, years after he was taken from his primate family, John tours with Africa's most respected children's choir, The Pearl of Africa.

He has apparently adapted to human life quite well. Consequently, John has been accused of being a fraud. Some say he made up his primitive past for attention and publicity.

But a BBC documentary crew recently captured evidence that suggests otherwise. They filmed John as he visited a group of vervet monkeys at a zoo and was able to communicate using guttural sounds and body language. After an hour or so, the foreign troop of monkeys accepted him into their group.

"It's the most fascinating case of a child being raised by wild animals," Ayp notes, "because he can move between the two worlds." ■

GIRLS RAISED BY WOLVES?

Though rare, there are other stories about feral children, that is, children being raised by animals in the wild for short periods. The most notable of these is the case of Kamala and Amala, two young Indian girls who were allegedly raised by wolves for several years.

When these girls were found in 1920, Amala was about 3 and Kamala was 8. Rescuers discovered them living inside a wolf den south of Calcutta where they reportedly had to pull the girls from the embrace of a pair of wolf cubs. The girls were not sisters, and it was assumed they were taken separetely by the wolves.

For a while, the girls behaved like wolves, running on all fours, eating raw meat, and staying active at nighttime. The younger girl died, most likely from bacteria in the uncooked meat she had been eating. Kamala slowly (and never fully) adapated to human life.

DOG TALK

BY GUSTAF GROWL, ANIMAL BEHAVIORIST

While you might not have been raised by wolves, you can learn how to communicate with their closest living relative: the dog. Dogs communicate with each other using mostly nonverbal cues, in other words, they use their bodies, not their voices, to get their feelings across.

HERE ARE SOME WAYS TO UNDERSTAND WHAT YOUR DOG MIGHT BE SAYING TO YOU:

"Bowing" dog (front legs bent to the ground, back legs straight): This is play position. This dog is inviting you to play with him!

Tail wagging in upward arched position, relaxed stance: This is a happy dog.

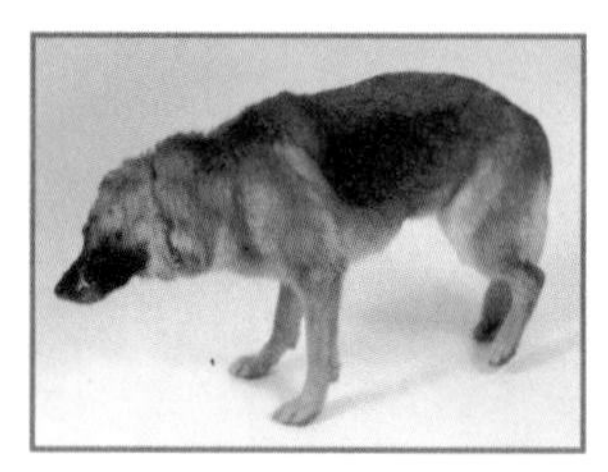

Ears folded back: Scared, fearful, or angry.

Arched back: Scared, fearful. Also goes hand-in-hand with prickled fur.

Tail between the legs: Scared, anxious.

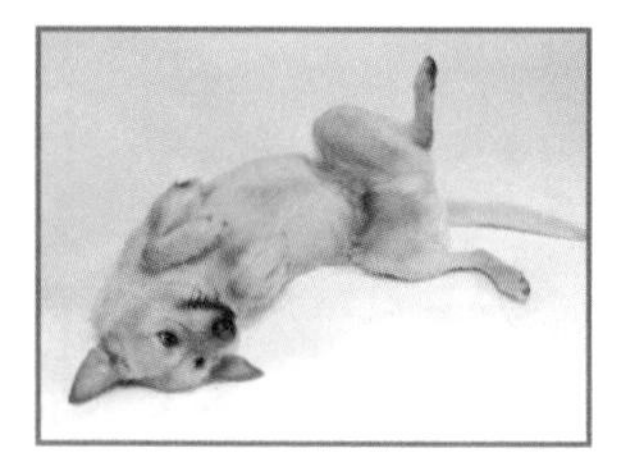

Lying on back, belly bared: Submissive.

Snarled lips: Angry, defensive. This dog wants you to back away.

MR. DICTIONARY SAYS . . .

Feral: Not domesticated; having become wild.

The Mysterious Times

February 29, 2000 | Volume LIV No. 8 | Price: One Dollar

IS THAT A BLACK HOLE IN THE SKY?

IMAGES REVEAL COMPELLING NEW EVIDENCE

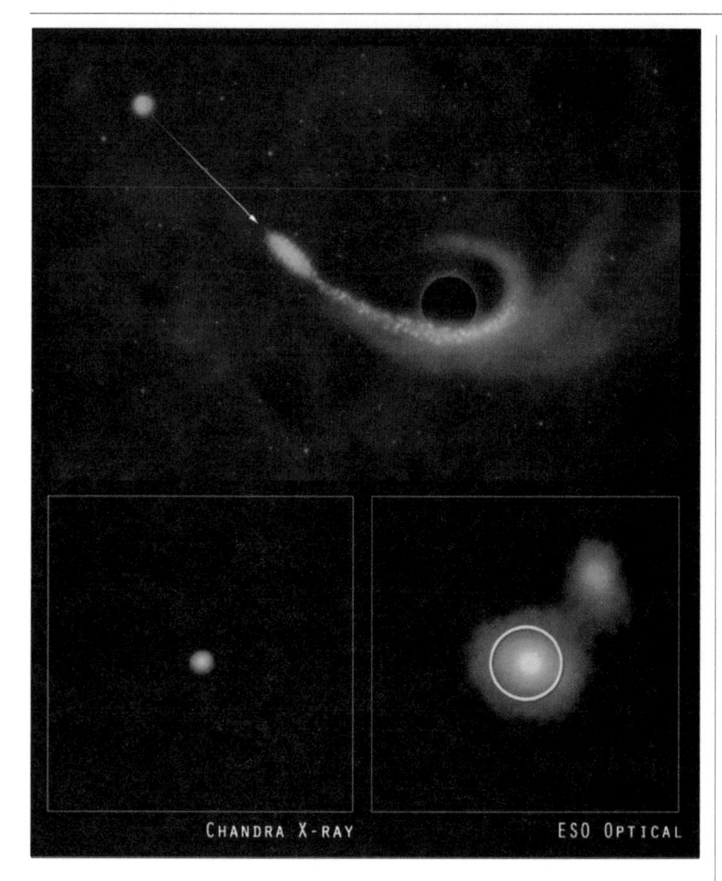

Left: *A giant black hole rips a star apart.*

CAMBRIDGE, MASSACHUSSETTS After decades of battling charges of science-fiction, scientists say they have acquired the most compelling evidence that black holes—invisible, gravity-filled whirlpools that suck up anything that comes too close—are real.

The proof, they say, lies in the discoveries made by NASA's Chandra X-ray Observatory, a massive telescope launched in 1999 and run out of the Harvard-Smithsonian Center for Astrophysics in Cambridge. Scientists say the telescope recently captured numerous images of what they think is a massive black hole gobbling up space matter smack in the middle of the Milky Way.

Admittedly the high-tech telescope didn't get pictures of the black hole itself, since by definition a black hole is invisible. Instead the images show a series of X-ray flares given off by the suspected black hole. In the images, the X-rays look like brilliant white lights magnified amidst the dark, starry sky.

Astronomers call the images clear evidence.

"These images prove that black holes are not a thing of fiction," asserts astronomy professor Derek Skycam. "This is the closest we've come to seeing one of outer space's biggest secrets."

Black holes are invisible, scientists say, because their gravity is so strong that they suck up anything around them—including light.

"Just like anything you throw into the air is going to get pulled back to the ground, anything that gets too close to a black hole is going to be sucked inside," Skycam said. "You can't see black holes because all the light around them has been sucked up."

Black holes form when a massive star, one that's at least 10 to 15 times bigger than our sun, runs out of fuel and can no longer support its weight. The star collapses, its weight pushing it into a smaller and smaller space while giving it more and more energy. Eventually the star shrinks to about the size of an atom and its gravitational pull grows bigger than ever.

The outer edge of a black hole is called its "event horizon," and is considered the point of no return. As for the inside of the black hole, which is called its "singularity," not much is known. It has been hypothesized that it could be a tunnel into other universes or times, but most scientists say that's unlikely.

The modern search for black holes began in the 1960s with physicist John Wheeler. At the time his theory was a controversial one,

(continued on page 2)

(continued from page 1)
since many scientists were reluctant to accept something they couldn't actually see. But astronomers have been scouring the skies for evidence ever since, looking at objects through telescopes.

When these observations revealed a star moving irregularly, they theorized that the strange movement was being caused by the nearby forces of a black hole. In addition, since materials that are sucked into black holes are said to emit X-rays, scientists used special telescopes to detect them.

And contrary to science-fiction lore, it's not likely that the Earth, the sun, or any exploring astronauts will be sucked into a black hole.

According to physicist Anna Eppanova, "You'd have to be sitting right next to a black hole to be sucked inside. I think if we were that close to one we'd have already found it." ■

Above: *Chandra's powerful telescope reveals that not all black holes spin at the same rate.*

WIN A TRIP INTO A BLACK HOLE!

Scientists aren't exactly sure what would happen if a person or probe were to enter the high-gravity realm of a black hole. That's why they're asking YOU to help them out. INSANE SPACECORPS, a new space exploration organization founded by a New York City middle-school science teacher, is seeking one brave soul to put on a space suit and explore a black hole up close and personal!

SOUND DANGEROUS? "It most definitely is!" says one expert. But that's not stopping INSANE SPACECORPS from trying!

ADVENTURERS: If you'd like to win an all-expenses-paid trip to a black hole, all you've got to do is write a 99,000-word essay including the following information about yourself: your spacecraft navigation skills; the approximate amount of time you can hold your breath; and your expected reaction to the black hole's high-gravity environment.

CONTACT INSANE SPACECORPS, 555-BLACK-HOLE FOR MORE INFORMATION.

WHAT'S IN A LEAP YEAR?

BY HOLLY DAY

Today is a rare day in the modern calendar. Not only is this year a leap year, which adds an extra day—February 29—to make 366 days in the year; it is also a centesimal year, or a year ending in '00.

Leap years occur once every four years, with the exclusion of centesimal years; only one in every four centesimal years are leap years. That means the last centesimal leap year happened in February 1600, and the next one won't occur until 2400.

The next regular leap year will occur four years from now, in 2004.

Leap years were added during Roman times as a trick to keep our calendar in line with the Earth's revolutions. Without them each year would be about six hours too long, making the seasons appear as if they're changing too soon. Imagine a hot summer day in New York City . . . in February. In other words, leap years keep our seasons constant with our calendars.

(continued from page 1)

Scientists say that if there were living organisms on Mars when those rocks were formed, the conditions would have allowed the organisms to survive. But they're not talking about little green men. While scientists hypothesize the planet might once have hosted life, they say it most likely was in the form of microscopic organisms, like bacteria. No actual fossilized evidence of such bacteria has been found on the Martian surface, but scientists plan to continue the search.

"Even with water flowing, the Martian environment was pretty unlivable," Anett said. "It would have been like living in Antarctica, but colder. That's how tough it would be to survive."

Today, the conditions on Mars, located about 34 million miles (54.4 million km) from Earth, are totally inhospitable to life as we know it. The planet has no atmospheric oxygen, which organisms on Earth need to breathe. There's also no ozone layer, which is necessary to protect living things from the Sun's ultraviolet (UV) rays. The average temperature on Mars is about –64 degrees Fahrenheit (–53 degrees C). Scientists say it's possible there's ice hidden below the surface of the planet, but none has yet been found.

"We've only explored a tiny piece of this planet," said physicist Peter T. Microbe. "This is just the beginning." Of course, finding any form of life, even tiny traces of bacteria, increases the chances that other extraterrestrial life forms exist." Microbe added, "If life has developed on two planets in our solar system, it could happen somewhere else, on other planets in other galaxies. We can't be the only ones."

According to a *Mysterious Times* poll, about half of those polled believe life once existed on Mars. Almost 75 percent said they believe life exists elsewhere.

"Thinking we're the only ones is a little selfish," said San Francisco eighth-grader B. Astro Nott. "Space is a pretty big place. It'd be a shame to waste it all on us." ■

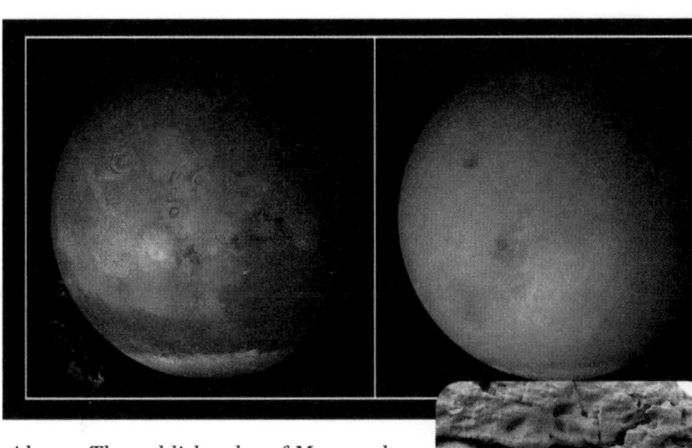

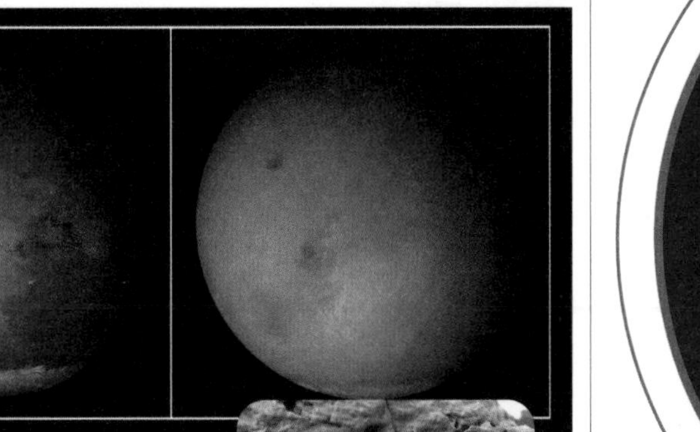

Above: *The reddish color of Mars makes it easy to identify. However, dust storms sometimes cover most of the planet (see right), making its distinctive color hazy.* Right: *A close-up of the surface of Mars.*

MARTIAN FACTS

Mars is the fourth planet from the Sun, the next beyond Earth.

It revolves around the Sun once every 687 Earth days.

The length of a Martian day is 24 hours, 39 minutes, and 35 seconds.

It's windy! Surface winds can move up to 80 miles per hour (130 kph).

Temperatures average –64 degrees Fahrenheit (–53 degrees C).

Gravity is 38 percent of Earth's gravity.

Mars has two moons: Phobos and Deimos.

Its atmosphere is 95.3 percent carbon dioxide, 2.7 percent nitrogen, and 1.6 percent argon.

TO LEARN MORE: Check out NASA's Mars website: HTTP://MARS.JPL.NASA.GOV/

WHY SO RED?

BY GUEST ASTRONOMER PROFESSOR NIGHTSKY

If you look up into the night sky, you can spot Mars even without a telescope because it looks slightly reddish when compared to Venus—also visible in the night sky—and other stars.

But why is it red? Much of Mars is thought to be covered with iron-rich dust and rocks that have oxidized, or rusted, much like metal gets rusty and reddish after time.

The Mysterious Times

March 3, 2004 Volume LVIII No. 10 Price: One Dollar

LIFE MAY HAVE EXISTED ON MARS

PLANET'S SURFACE WAS ONCE "DRENCHED," SCIENTISTS SAY

WASHINGTON, D.C. — Is there life on Mars? Scientists now believe it is possible, even likely.

Shortly after finishing a 90-day mission to the Red Planet, the rover *Opportunity*, one of two high-tech robots sent by NASA to explore the harsh Martian terrain, sent back pictures of what appears be a dried-up lake bed, suggesting that the planet might have at one time been wet enough for living things to flourish. "Where there's water, there's life," said planetary scientist Paul Anett. "If Mars was once flowing with water, it was probably once flowing with living things."

NASA sent *Opportunity* and another rover called *Spirit* to Mars about three months ago. The goal of the mission was to find out whether the planet, which is now a dry, cold expanse of canyons and craters, ever had the type of environment that could support life.

"Every living organism that we know of—down to the smallest of bacteria—needs water to survive," said biologist Mike R. Scope. "This discovery may be the answer to the long-standing question: Is there life on other planets?"

Scientists analyzed a particular area of rock and found evidence of sulfates and other minerals that can form only in or around water. "The presence of those minerals can only mean water once flowed there," Scope explained.

(continued on page 2)

Above: *High-tech robot explores Mars' terrain.* Below: *Dried-up lake bed suggests there was once life on Mars.*

IN OTHER NEWS

✦ HUMAN CLONES ✦ ON THE WAY?
Scientists in South Korea reportedly cloning 30 human embryos. See INNOVATIONS.

✦ DESTINATION LIBYA! ✦
United States ends ban on travel to Libya after 23 years of restrictions. See TRAVEL.

✦ DOGGIE TOILETS? ✦
No need for a pooper scooper? Dogs in Amsterdam are testing the new "doggie toilet," a small fenced-in patch of grass that self-cleans after each use. See PETS.